NATHANAEL-ISRAEL ISRAEL, PhD

I0520592

HOW GOD CREATED BABY UNIVERSE

OTHER BOOKS BY NATHANAEL-ISRAEL ISRAEL

Get them at your local bookstore, or online (e.g. on Amazon, Science180.com/books)

Turbulent Origin of the Universe
There is Only One Scientific, Simple, Safe, Trustworthy, Unexpensive, Brave, Practical, Nonconformist, Universal, Verifiable Formula that Accurately Decodes the Universe Formation ... But You Are Not Using It

Reconciling Science and Creation Accurately
What Science Accurately Teaches about Creation and God's Existence that Atheists, Freethinkers, and even Most Christians Ignore ... And How to Demonstrate it Without Taking Sides Between Rationality and Faith

Turbulent Origin of Chemical Particles
Why You Don't Have to Embrace Evolution, Big Bang, or Deny God to Scientifically Prove the Formation of All Chemical Particles

Origin of the Spiritual World
Top Secrets about the Origin of Everything in the Universe that Some Elites Have Hidden from You for Thousands of Years

From Science to Bible's Conclusions
How Decoding the Universe-Origin by Properly Revisiting Scientific Data—That Top Scientists Collected but Wrongly Analyzed—Bizarrely led to the 3500 Years Old Biblical Account of Creation

Turbulent Origin of Life
Why You Don't Have to Embrace Evolutionism or Check Your Brain at the Door in the Name of Faith or Science to Accurately Decrypt the Origin of Life Using the Historic Formula of the Universe Formation

How Baby Universe Was Born
How to Scientifically Talk to Children about the Universe Formation and They will Know Forever How to Correctly Test the Intersection of Science and Faith

Science180 Accurate Scientific Proof of God
Can We Scientifically Explain the Formation of the Universe Through Natural Processes Without Evoking Evolution and Big Bang?

Mathematical Proof of God's Existence at the Intersection of Science and Faith.
The Scientifically Verifiable Cosmological Theory that Challenges the Big Bang Theory at the Crossroads of Reason and Religion THEY Want You to Ignore

More books written by Nathanael-Israel Israel can be found at Israel120.com/books

NATHANAEL-ISRAEL ISRAEL, PhD

Discoverer of the Universe Turbulent Origin Formula
Discoverer of the Scientific Formula of the Existence of God
Founder of Science180, www.Science180.com

HOW GOD CREATED BABY UNIVERSE

What Children Must Scientifically Learn Early about the Universe Formation to Avoid Dangerously Abandoning God Later in Life Just Like Most College Students Who Embrace Evolution and Big Bang That Deny Biblical Creation

Science180

Augusta
United States of America
www.Science180Publishing.com

How God Created Baby Universe
What Children Must Scientifically Learn Early about the Universe Formation to Avoid
Dangerously Abandoning God Later in Life Just Like Most College Students Who Embrace
Evolution and Big Bang That Deny Biblical Creation

First edition: October 2025

Published by Science180
Augusta (USA)
www.Science180Publishing.com

Book Cover and Illustrations by Nathanael-Israel Israel

ISBN: 979-8-9932150-7-5

Library of Congress Control Number: 2025920948

CONTENT

SECTION 1: INTRODUCTION

Science180: The All-In-One Proven & Uncomplicated Universe-Origin and Life-Origin Formula

1. Who am I, and why this fantastic book?

- How was the universe formed?
- How were the Sun and all the stars in the universe formed?
- How were the Earth and all the other planets in the universe formed?
- How were the Moon and the other satellites in the universe formed?
- Is there any book that presents a nice story of the formation of the universe that both children and their parents can read and enjoy together as a family?
- How can children quickly know for sure which story of the origin of the universe is trustworthy and correct?
- Is there any story on the origin of the universe that can prepare children for a better tomorrow?
- How can children correct wrong stories about the origin of the universe so they and their parents can save time and money, and improve their lives?
- How can children be trained to properly answer deep questions about the formation of the Earth, Moon, and Sun that even some highly educated people ignore?
- Can children use mathematics and science to test whether God created the universe as the Bible says?
- How can children use science to prove that God exists?
- How can we properly explain all these difficult things to children in simple language that they can easily understand and enjoy?

If you are interested in finding the correct answer to any of these questions and others related to the origin of the universe and everything in it, including the planets, stars, satellites, and even life, then you have found the perfect book written for great people like you.

Welcome to the well-known book about how the universe was born. As you read this book, I am sure you will learn a lot about how the universe began. Before I start telling the story, let me tell you a little bit about myself.

My name is Josephine Israel. I am 10 years old. I have a sister (Joelle-Major Israel) and a brother (Joshua-Enoch Israel). My little sister is 9, and my little brother is 7. We are all born and raised in the United States of America. We are in elementary school.

At this point, please let me introduce you to my Daddy, the one who wrote this book. Indeed, Dad is a scientist, writer, and businessperson. He has spent many years studying and researching how the universe was formed. He discovered many great things about the origin of the universe, which means how the universe was formed. He published some of those things in 9 books in 2025:

- "Turbulent Origin of the Universe" (written for scientists: people who study science)

SECTION 1: INTRODUCTION

- "Reconciling Science and Creation Accurately" (written for Christians and anyone else who wants to learn how science properly proves the Biblical creation)
- "Turbulent Origin of Chemical Particles" (written for chemists: people who study chemicals)
- "From Science to Bible's Conclusions" (written for the general public: everybody, even the nonscientists)
- "Turbulent Origin of Life" (written for biologists (people who study biology or life science) and for anyone else who wants to understand how life was formed)
- "Origin of the Spiritual World" (written for those who want to understand deep stuff related to the spiritual world)
- "Science180 Accurate Scientific Proof of God" (written for anyone interested in scientifically knowing whether God exists or not)

I am not surprised that people tell my dad he is the #1 international authority who truly helps people properly unlock the secrets of the turbulence that shaped the universe. He is acknowledged as the world's most accurate universe-origin scientist and the world's most trusted expert who properly decoded the formation of the universe, life, and chemicals. Some people referred to him as the undisputable specialist of all questions at the intersection of science and Biblical creation. He is the "Creator of Science180 Academy" (www.Science180Academy.com). He is the "Creator of the Universe Turbulent Origin Formula," the "Discoverer of the Universe Creation Formula." He has had the honor of being recognized as the first human being to scientifically reconcile science with the Biblical account of creation. Some people call him the outside-of-the-box universe-origin scientist and the world's most accurate universe-origin mathematician. Although he is called by many other names, my siblings and I are glad to call him Daddy or Dad. Therefore, in the rest of this book, I will just call him by these two names.

Unfortunately, as of 2023, none of these books I mentioned above were written for children like us. Therefore, Dad decided to share with us what he has discovered about the formation of the universe in a language that children can understand. I am very proud of him and happy that he has spent 3 years working with us, his children, to break down complex scientific concepts into a language you and I can understand.

Because we were happy with his children's lessons on the origin of the universe, we decided to share them with the whole world rather than keep them just for ourselves. In other words, Dad thought it would be even better to write a children's book about how the universe was formed so that children our age across the globe can understand and enjoy together with their parents. That is how this book was born and written during the summer break of 2023, precisely between July and August 2023. Then, we reviewed it again during the summer break of 2024. Then, we waited for another year before releasing it to the whole world.

Science180: The All-In-One Proven & Uncomplicated Universe-Origin and Life-Origin Formula

In this book, I will be leading my little sister and brother to share with you great information about how Baby Universe was born. Later, we will do some math to calculate how long it took for the Earth, the Moon, and the Sun to be formed. Then we will see whether that story really matches what the Bible or other books say. I am sure you will enjoy the story.

The first children's book that my dad wrote about the origin of the universe was for people, including Christians who believe in God or who want to know about how He created the universe. Hence, he named that book *"How God Created Baby Universe."* That is the book you are reading now. This book is divided into 2 parts. The first part deals with pure science that children can completely enjoy, and the second part answers many questions that smart children and their parents usually ask about God. Two years after writing that book, my dad realized that some people who don't believe in God and who are really interested in the origin of the universe may not read it because the title contains the word "God." Therefore, to help those people at least understand how the scientific data points to God, Dad decided to remove the second part of this book (which talks about God) and make the title and remaining information appeal to those who deny God. He called that book *"How Baby Universe Was Born."* And it is for children ages 7-12 who don't or whose parents don't believe in God. By the end of that book written toward unbelievers, Dad also still showed how his demonstration points to God. Then he informed readers of the existence of this book, which contains the entire story of how science explains how God created the universe. That way, people who want to know the full story can still refer to this book you are reading.

Dad said that it is very important that believers learn to reach out to those who deny God by presenting the message in a language that unbelievers can understand and readily accept, rather than insulting them for rejecting God.

Everybody wants to know about the universe, and I am glad that my dad has found a way to introduce his cool discovery to everybody, including curious children like us. In other words, if you believe in God but don't know how to demonstrate the way He created the universe in a language that children can understand, and if you are looking for a book that scientifically shows children how God created the whole universe, then this book is for you.

This amazing book you are reading is the first to present how the scientific data collected by top scientists across the globe, including at NASA, perfectly match the Biblical story of the creation of the Earth, the Moon, and the Sun. This book definitely presents the origin story in a style that challenges children like us to think creatively. Without waiting any longer, just relax, and let's talk about how we came up with the first questions of this book!

2. Very important questions about the universe's formation

After Dad decided to write the book for children like us, he ensured we would like

SECTION 1: INTRODUCTION

it. To be sure he would answer all of our questions, Dad gave us a week to come up with the questions we had about how the universe was formed. Many very important questions quickly came to mind, but we were not able to answer them properly, and we were not even sure our answers were correct. By the way, every time I use the word "we", please know that I am talking about my little brother, my sister, and me. To the surprise of our dad, within a few days, we came up with more than 100 great and very big questions that we wanted to understand:

1. How was Baby Earth born?
2. Who was Baby Earth's mother?
3. How old is the Earth?
4. How was the Moon formed?
5. How were all the planets formed?
6. How were the stars formed?
7. Why does the Moon turn around the Earth?
8. Why does the Earth turn around the Sun?
9. Why does the Sun give light while the Earth does not?
10. How were the seas and the oceans made?
11. How was the sky made?
12. Why are the planets different?
13. Why are some planets gaseous, others solid, and some icy?
14. Why do planets have different colors?
15. How were plants made?
16. Why are most plants green?
17. How were animals made?
18. How were people made?
19. How many creatures are there in the universe?
20. Why do birds fly, but people cannot fly?
21. How was the air we breathe made, and where do clouds come from?
22. Why is there light and darkness, and where do they come from?
23. How can we use science to prove that God really created the universe as the Bible says?
24. Who and where is God?
25. Who made Him?
26. What does He look like?
27. How old is God?
28. Is it true that God created everything?
29. How did God make the galaxies?
30. Why does the Bible say that it took six days for God to create everything?
31. How did God make heaven?
32. What does heaven look like?
33. Where was God before creation?
34. Why can't we live forever like God?

Science180: The All-In-One Proven & Uncomplicated Universe-Origin and Life-Origin Formula

35. When God spoke for things to appear during creation, where did they come from?
36. When God created Adam and Eve, what did they look like?
37. Before God created Adam and Eve, what was the universe like, and what was God Himself like?
38. When the animals were created, did they obey God's instructions?
39. Did God create any bad animals that may have hurt people?
40. How come everybody does not believe in God? Etc.

These questions are very important, and we need to know their answers so we can be smarter. As we presented these questions to Dad, he was happy because he felt like they were really HUGE problems. Although these questions are very hard for children our age, Dad said he will do his best to help us overcome any obstacles that may try to prevent us from understanding them. If you have ever asked any of these questions or are interested in learning about them, you are in the right place.

Throughout my writing, wherever you see "universe-origin," please know that I meant "origin of the universe" or "the origin of the universe." Likewise, wherever you see "life-origin," please understand that I meant "origin of life" or "the origin of life." In the same manner, wherever I mention "chemicals-origin," please know that I am referring to "origin of chemicals" or "the origin of chemicals." Moreover, I will be posting some interesting kids' content online, and you can find it at www.Science180.com/children.

In the rest of this book, I will share with you what my siblings and I have learned from Dad about how the universe was formed. Do you want to get started with some fun stuff that will make you laugh a lot? If yes, let's go!

SECTION 2: HOW THE GALAXIES, THE PLANETS, THE MOON, AND THE SUN WERE FORMED

3. Important things in the Solar System

When I look in the sky, I see the stars, the moon, the clouds, some planets, and the Sun. I learned that all of those stars, planets, and moons are moving in space without anything holding them. I learned that each of them was created on a specific date. As I was curious, I asked Daddy, "How was the Earth made?"

Daddy told me that to better explain how the Earth was formed, he first needed to tell me certain things about the Earth.

The Solar System (see Figure 1) is the name by which the Sun and everything that orbits the Sun are called. In other words, the Solar System is a group or family of celestial bodies made of the Sun and the bodies that orbit the Sun. The Earth is one of the many planets in the Solar System. To explain how the Earth was made, Daddy said he also needed to explain how the W-H-O-L-E Solar System was made.

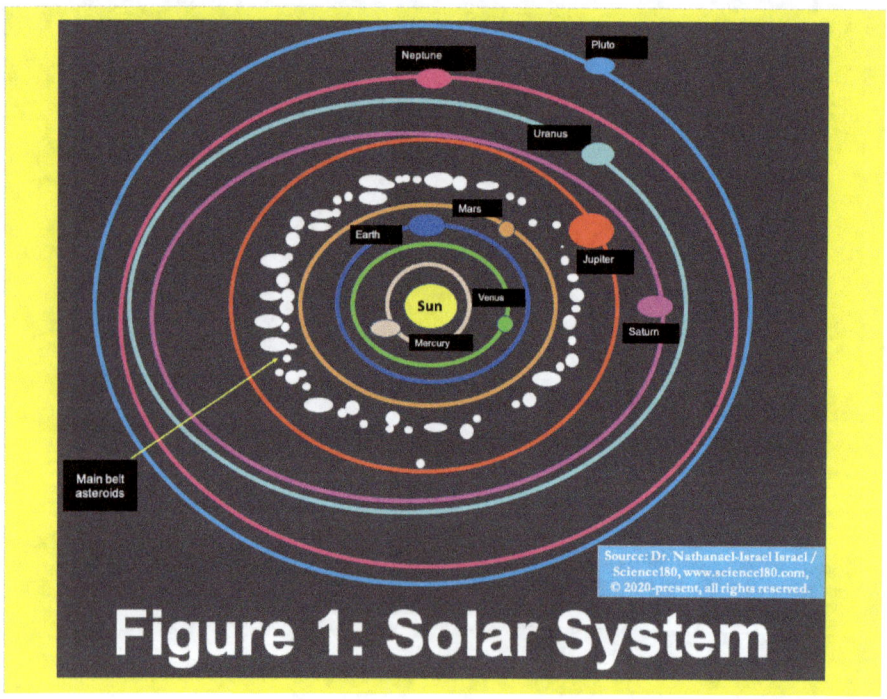

Figure 1: Solar System

For thousands of years, people have tried to explain how the Solar System was made, and they have come up with many ideas. I will not go over all of those ideas with you because you may not understand them, as they involve a lot of math, a lot of thinking, and a lot of guessing, which is hard to believe. But I will tell you what I learned from Dad, who spent many years to figure out how the WHOLE universe was formed. Let's first look at certain things in the Solar System.

The Sun, the Earth, the Moon, and all of the other planets in the Solar System

Nathanael-Israel Israel: Known as the World's Most Accurate Universe-Origin Mathematician

are called celestial bodies. In other words, a celestial body is a big natural object like a planet or a star in the sky.

The Sun is the biggest celestial body in the Solar System. The Sun is almost 1000 times as big as Earth. The Earth is a planet. The other planets in the Solar System are Mercury, Venus, Mars, Jupiter, Saturn, Uranus, and Neptune. For a long time, Pluto was considered a planet, but for a few years, some people haven't considered it a planet anymore. However, in many books, you will see Pluto still considered a planet. Old people who learned the names of the planets a long time ago will still tell you that Pluto is a planet. Therefore, forgive me or anybody else if sometimes I or they also consider Pluto a planet.

The Sun is located almost in the middle of the Solar System. All of the other celestial bodies in the Solar System are moving around the Sun, and each of them is located at a specific distance. Some are very close to the Sun, and others are very far away, but all of them are located millions of miles from the Sun and from one another. Mercury is the closest planet to the Sun.

Certain planets have other celestial bodies turning around them. For example, the Moon turns around the Earth (see Figure 2).

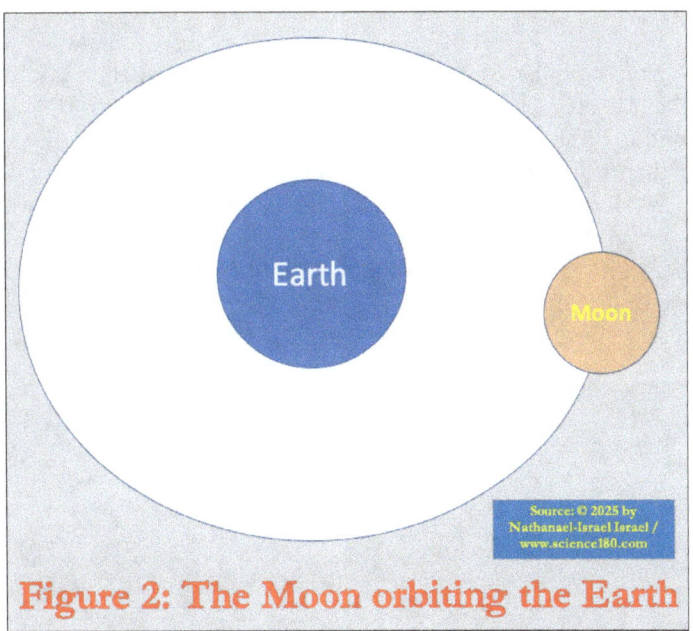

Figure 2: The Moon orbiting the Earth

A celestial body that orbits a planet is called a satellite. Some planets do not have even a single satellite. For instance, Mercury and Venus do not have a satellite.

Some celestial bodies turn around the Sun but are not satellites. Most of them are called asteroids, and all of them are smaller than the planets. For instance, between Mars and Jupiter is the main asteroid belt, which contains millions of asteroids (see Figure 3).

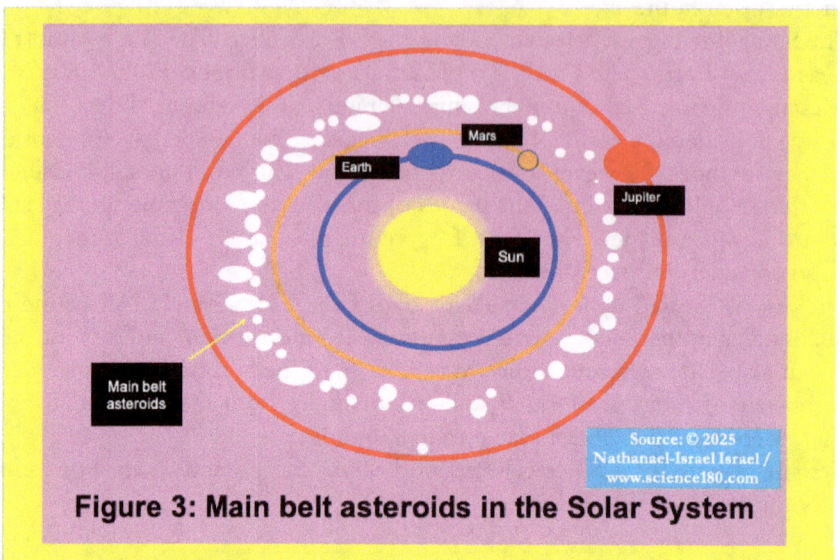

Figure 3: Main belt asteroids in the Solar System

Each body in the Solar System is different. Some are small, and others are big. The Sun is the biggest celestial body in the Solar System. Jupiter is the biggest planet moving around the Sun. Mars and Pluto are the smallest planets. Jupiter is about 10 times bigger than the Earth. Some planets move fast, and some move slowly. The fastest planet is Mercury, and the slowest planet is Pluto. For those who think Pluto is no longer a planet, we can say that Neptune is the slowest planet. Neptune is the planet just before Pluto. Daddy told me that from Mercury all the way to Neptune and Pluto, the speed of the planets decreases, meaning it slows as the distance from the Sun increases. See Figure 4 for more details.

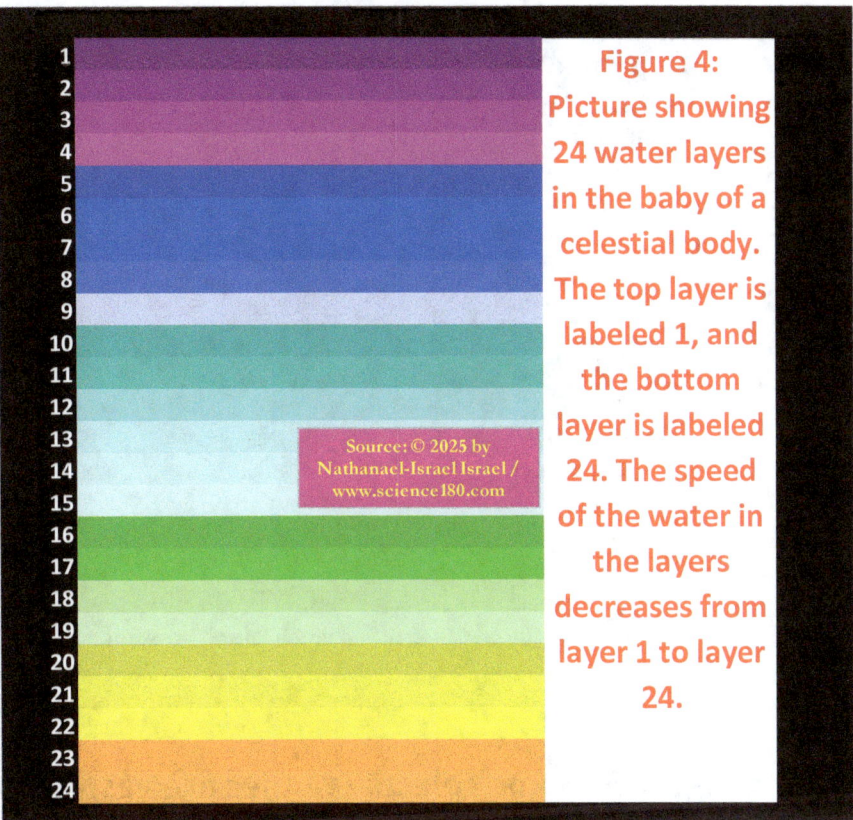

Figure 4: Picture showing 24 water layers in the baby of a celestial body. The top layer is labeled 1, and the bottom layer is labeled 24. The speed of the water in the layers decreases from layer 1 to layer 24.

Source: © 2025 by Nathanael-Israel Israel / www.science180.com

The celestial bodies in the Solar System are made of different materials. Some are very hot, and others are very cold. For example, the Sun is the HOTTEST celestial body in the Solar System, and the farther we get from the Sun, the colder things get. In other words, the celestial bodies that are FAR away from the Sun are colder than those close to the Sun. Some celestial bodies in the Solar System are solid, some are ice, and some are gas. By the way, the gas I'm talking about here is not the gas we put in our cars or the air we release when we use the bathroom. Thank goodness, or else those celestial bodies made up of gas would be STINKY! The Earth is a very solid planet. Jupiter is an example of a gas giant. Uranus is a planet that is filled with ice, like the ice we get from the freezer on a hot summer day (Figure 5).

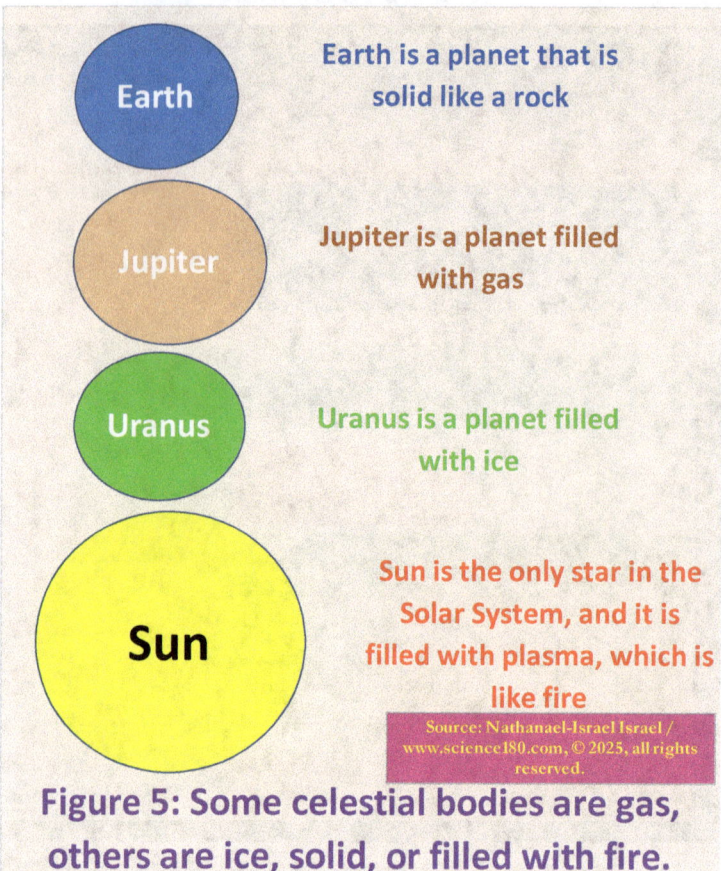

Earth is a planet that is solid like a rock

Jupiter is a planet filled with gas

Uranus is a planet filled with ice

Sun is the only star in the Solar System, and it is filled with plasma, which is like fire

Figure 5: Some celestial bodies are gas, others are ice, solid, or filled with fire.

The Sun is not a planet but a star. It is filled with very HOT materials like lava, fire, steam, and something Daddy calls plasma. Lava and plasma are like the hot material that flows out of the Earth from volcanoes. Daddy told me that each planet has some lava inside. Although it shines, the Moon is not a star. It receives light from the Sun and sends it back to Earth. In fact, just as a light hitting a mirror is pushed or thrown back into another direction, so also when the light coming from the Sun hits the surface of the Moon, it is sent back to the Earth. You can do this experiment by shining a flashlight onto a mirror. You will see how the light is sent in another direction. To say that the light is sent into another direction, scientists use the term "reflected." In other words, when the light coming from the Sun hits the surface of the Moon, it is reflected to the Earth.

Unlike us, who stand up straight as we walk, all planets stand straight as they move around the Sun. Some are almost straight, and others are bent or leaning. Some are bent more than others. Some are even upside down, as if they were walking on their heads rather than their feet. Some are even rolling like a soccer ball rolling on the ground. Jupiter is almost straight.

Figure 6: Axial tilt of some planets in the Solar System

The Earth is a little bit bent. Uranus moves like it is rolling like a somersault, whereas Venus is upside down as if it were moving on its head, which is weird. Scientists use the big work called "axis tilt" to determine how bent or tilted the planets are. Figure 6 shows the axis tilt of the planets in the Solar System.

Science180: All the Universe-Origin and Life-Origin Solutions You Love

HOW GOD CREATED BABY UNIVERSE

I asked my dad why he was telling us all of this stuff that is making me think more than the small question we asked in the beginning. My dad told me to cool down, and he will very soon explain to us (meaning my sister, my brother, and me) why the planets are behaving like that, for all of their attitudes or the way they are acting is linked to how they were made.

By the time Daddy reached this part of the story, we were very excited and couldn't wait until he answered the HUGE questions running through our minds:

- Why is the Sun very big and very hot?
- Why are some planets slow and others fast?
- Why are some planets made with ice, some with gas, and some solid like the Earth?
- How come the planets are not the same?
- Why are the planets located at different distances?
- How did the planets get there?
- Where did they come from?
- Why does the Sun contain some hot materials like lava, and why do some planets also have the same on the inside?
- Are the planets, which are cold, made of ice cream that we can eat?

As I asked those questions to Daddy, he smiled at me and said: "*You are a very smart girl.*" He added that those questions are exactly part of what needs to be explained to address how the Solar System was formed to kids my age. By this time, I felt very happy because I knew Daddy would explain to us how everything in the universe was created. I hope you are following what I am saying, because very soon I will explain everything to you.

My daddy has written many books about how the universe was made, but they are too difficult for a little child like me to understand. That is why he decided to break the story down for us in a simple way that we could understand. Now, I am going to share with you what we learned. Daddy did not tell me everything that happened during the formation of the universe, but what a child like me can understand without having to learn difficult things that people who went to school for many, many years have learned. If you are ready, let's go!

**Nathanael-Israel Israel: Known as the World's Most Accurate Universe-
Origin Mathematician**

4. Beginning of Baby Solar System

Everything in the universe has a beginning. Just as a baby is born, grows, lies still, crawls, walks, runs, and jumps before starting school and learning different things, so also the universe was born at one time and had to go through different changes so that everything in it could be formed and well-shaped as it grew. Just as a baby grows in height, weight, and strength, so also did things when they were being formed in the universe; they changed and took different forms.

Daddy told me that when he studied the universe, he realized that certain things are not the same or different by chance. For example, it is not by chance that the Sun is so big and contains hot things like lava, while inside the Earth, there is also lava that can produce volcanoes. All of this is because, at the beginning of the Solar System, there was something that looked like a Baby Solar System, which was very hot. Baby Solar System was a gigantic baby that was born and grew into the Solar System. By Baby Solar System, I am not talking about a small baby that you can hold in your hands, but a big thing that contained fires and, at one point, looked like a liquid or gas, let's say something Daddy called a fluid or plasma. A fluid is a liquid, such as water, or a gas, such as air. Unlike babies of human beings, who are small, Baby Solar System was very huge, and deep, and at one point, it was rich in something looking like water. Baby Solar System was not a human being, but something that went through many changes before becoming the Solar System. As Daddy continued the story, he said that, as it was being born, Baby Solar System was pushed by something and started moving very fast.

5. Mother Solar System birthed two babies

After a certain time, Baby Solar System grew up and became a mother who was pregnant and about to give birth to two children. Suddenly, Mother Solar System split into two parts: one became Baby Sun, and the other became the baby that would become every celestial body orbiting the Sun. In other words, Mother Solar System birthed two babies: Baby Sun and the baby of every celestial body moving around the Sun (see Figure 7). Baby Sun is the thing that grew, went through changes, and became the Sun. In the same way, the other baby that Mother Solar System birthed went through many changes and birthed all the bodies turning around the Sun.

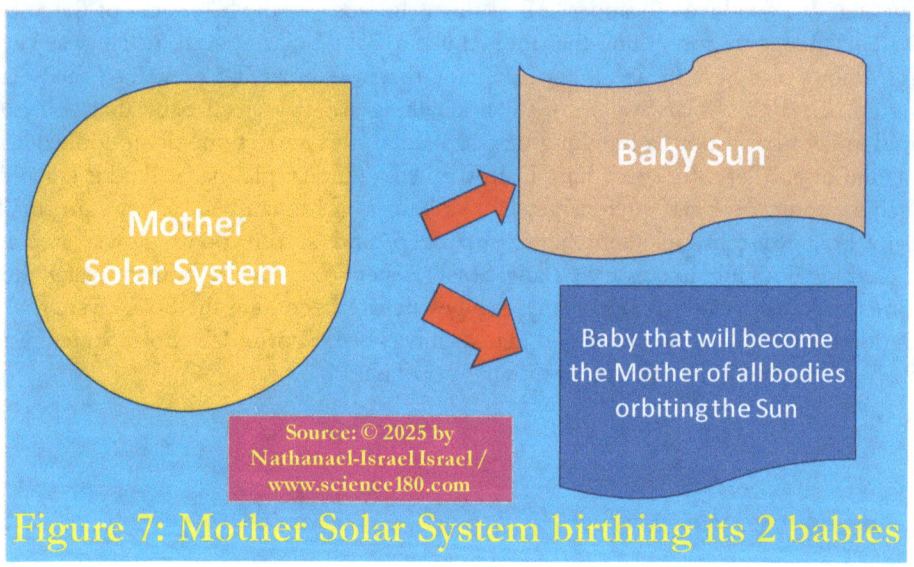

Figure 7: Mother Solar System birthing its 2 babies

All I am saying is just like in a family, a mommy gives birth to a baby who grows until it becomes an adult that gets married and gives birth to other children, and those children will also grow until they get married and give birth to other children. In the end, the family keeps growing, and we can end up having a grandpa who has children, grandchildren, great-grandchildren, and great-great-grandchildren. In the same manner, the babies of the bodies orbiting the Sun grew and birthed other babies. What I am saying about people in the family also applies to the celestial bodies in the Solar System. This is because Mother Solar System gave birth to two babies, which also, in their turn, grew up and birthed other babies. In fact, because Baby Sun was very huge, by the time it went through all of its changes, it had become a very huge Sun. I will explain those changes later. Before I get there, let me tell you something very important about the other Baby of the Mother Solar System. The other baby was not as big as Baby Sun. That Baby and Baby Sun were both in

16

SECTION 2: HOW THE GALAXIES, THE PLANETS, THE MOON, AND THE SUN WERE FORMED

the belly of Mother Solar System.

As Daddy reached this level of the story, I, Josephine, asked, "Daddy, how does a planet give birth to a baby when it does not have a belly?" Daddy answered by saying that when we talk about babies and mothers here, we are not talking about how a pregnant mother carries a baby in her womb for about 9 months before giving birth. But we are talking about how something like a liquid can break up or change forms to become another thing, which can also go through other changes to become something else. To demonstrate what he was saying, Daddy took us outside our house for an experiment on how water can break up into droplets. Keep reading to learn about this cool experiment.

6. A very important experiment of how water thrown into the air breaks into many moving water drops

How celestial bodies were born is different than how human beings are born. In fact, as baby celestial bodies were moving in space, one of the things that happened to them was that they turned around, and some pieces of the liquids they contained came off. To explain to us what happened during the formation of the universe, Daddy took a glass of water, took us outside, and threw the water into the air so we could observe or see what happens to it. We saw how the water broke into pieces, which moved in the direction Daddy threw it.

To be sure we understood the experiment, Daddy gave each of us a cup of water and a bucket of water, and let us put water in the cups and throw it into the air. We realized that when we threw the water into the air, it arched like a rainbow and broke into pieces that continued to move. Each piece had its own size and moved in its own direction according to the direction into which we threw the liquid. When we threw the water faster, the drops moved faster. We also noticed that some drops are bigger than others. Some drops went very far, and others feel close to us.

When Daddy took us outside for the water experiment, the water in the cup was like the mother water, which, when thrown into the air, gave rise to different water drops, which Daddy called Baby waters. It is almost like taking bubbles and blowing them from the wand into the air. Many Baby bubbles are born and move in the direction they were blown until some fall and others pop. In the same way, when the Mother Solar System was moving, it broke down into Baby Sun and into the Baby that will become all of the bodies turning around the Sun.

Just as some water drops were bigger than others, so also was the size of the babies of Mother Solar System different. In fact, the size of Baby Sun was more than 1000 times bigger than the size of the other Baby of the Mother Solar System. To make things easy, let's call Baby Sun, Baby 1, and let's call the Baby of all the bodies orbiting the sun Baby 2. In other words, Mother Solar System gave birth to two babies: Baby 1, which became the Sun, and Baby 2, which became the mother of all the bodies turning around the Sun (Figure 8).

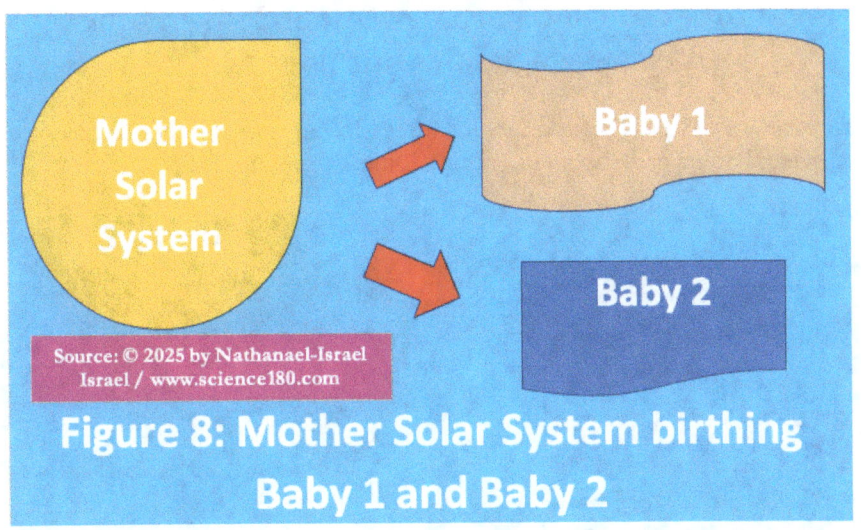

Source: © 2025 by Nathanael-Israel Israel / www.science180.com

Figure 8: Mother Solar System birthing Baby 1 and Baby 2

7. Baby 2 grew up and became Mother 2, the mother of all the celestial bodies orbiting the Sun

In the same way, Baby 2 started moving after Mother Solar System birthed it. As it was moving, Baby 2 grew up and became Mother 2 (see Figure 9).

Figure 9: Baby 2 grew up and became Mother 2

After Mother 2 traveled for a certain distance at a certain speed, it started giving birth to other babies. One of the first babies Mother 2 birthed was Baby Mercury (see Figure 10). This also explains why, in the end, Mercury is the planet closest to the Sun. After birthing Baby Mercury, Mother 2 continued moving away from the Sun.

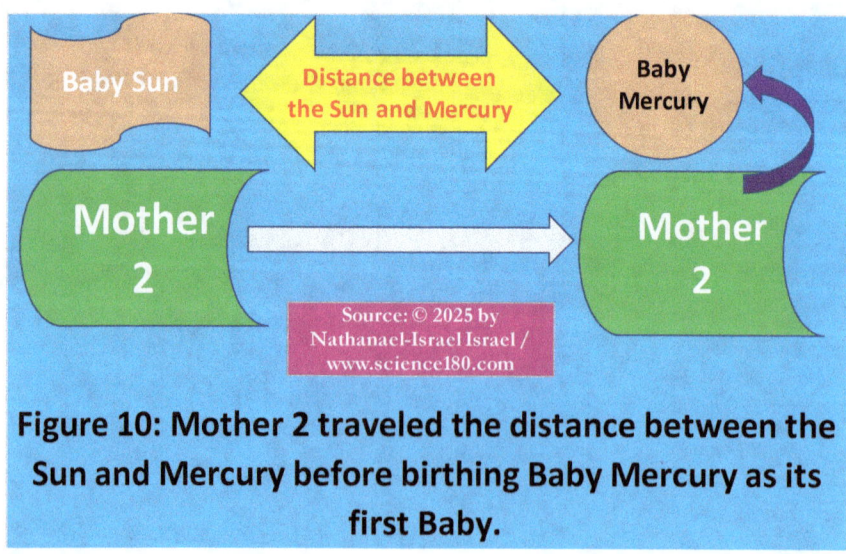

Figure 10: Mother 2 traveled the distance between the Sun and Mercury before birthing Baby Mercury as its first Baby.

When Daddy said this, I asked him, "Why did Baby 2, which became Mother 2, have to move away from Baby Sun?"

Daddy replied: "Do you remember the experiment we did for the water we threw into the air, and water drops were formed and moved?" I replied, "Yes." Daddy then told me that because Baby 2 was pushed away by Mother Solar System at a very high speed, it kept moving, and all of the babies it birthed after becoming Mother 2 also kept moving. Daddy continued the story by saying that Mother 2 kept moving away from Baby Sun, giving birth to different babies until it reached a point when it gave birth to another baby called Baby 3, which grew up to become the Mother of the Earth and the Moon. To make it simple, let's call Mother 3 the Mother of the Earth and the Moon. In other words, Mother 2 gave birth to Mother 3. As a reminder, Mother 2 was the mother of ALL celestial bodies turning around the Sun. The distance that Mother 2 traveled away from Baby Sun before giving birth to Mother 3 is about the distance separating the Earth from the Sun. Figure 11 shows that.

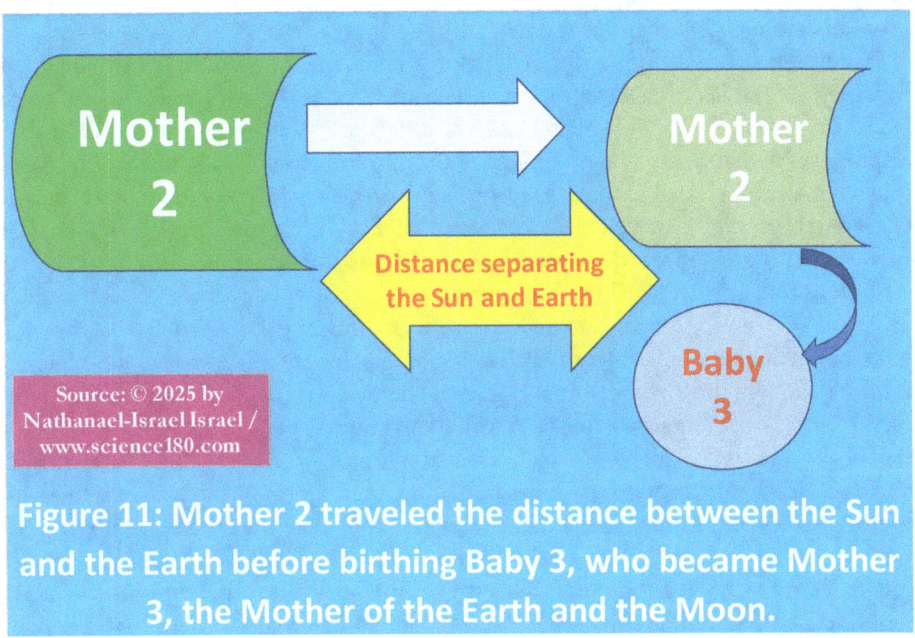

Figure 11: Mother 2 traveled the distance between the Sun and the Earth before birthing Baby 3, who became Mother 3, the Mother of the Earth and the Moon.

Daddy taught us that, using the speed at which Mother 2 moved and the distance between the Sun and the Earth, he calculated how long it took for Mother 3 (Mother of the Earth and the Moon) to form. We will get back to that later. For now, let's see how Mother 3 gave birth to its children.

8. Mother of the Earth and the Moon birthed Baby Earth and Baby Moon

The Mother of the Earth and the Moon, which Daddy called Mother 3, quickly gave birth to Baby Earth and Baby Moon. Baby Moon was much smaller than Baby Earth and was pushed away from Baby Earth. Baby Moon traveled for a certain distance before becoming the Adult Moon. Based on the great research that Daddy has done, the distance that Baby Moon traveled before forming the Adult Moon is about the distance separating the Earth and the Moon. That is why the Moon is far from Earth. After Baby Moon moved away from Baby Earth, Baby Earth went through some changes and became the Adult Earth that we call Earth today. Likewise, Baby Moon underwent some changes and became the Adult Moon we call the Moon today.

At this time of the story, my sister Joelle-Major raised her hand and asked Daddy: "What changes did Baby Earth, Baby Moon, and Baby Sun go through before becoming what they are today?"

Daddy replied that, unlike the babies of human beings who are born small and grow big, the Babies of celestial bodies are born huge and grow small. At this point, we all smiled and said: "WHAT?! How can that be?" We thought that ALL babies are born very small, and as they eat more food, they become bigger. Daddy replied to us that how celestial bodies are born and grow is different than how human Babies are born and grow. Babies of celestial bodies were born big, but as they were moving, they were squeezed or compressed and got smaller as small things inside of them were forming and making them harder. It is not exactly how you squeeze an orange to get orange juice, but it is because of how the liquid in the Babies was being organized inside to form different things, looking like spaghetti wrapped around a fork, as the Baby celestial bodies were trying to become adults (see Figure 12). In fact, as the liquid of the baby celestial bodies was trying to come together, they broke into small pieces, which moved around in circles like whirlwinds or tornadoes, spinning around at the same time they were being pressed to come together. In the end, they were small pieces of water here and there, compacted on their own, but put together as one body. "That is weird!" I responded. Daddy replied: "That's how it happened." This is like how inside a fruit, you can have some seeds and also some fleshy materials you can eat, and how all of them together form the fruit.

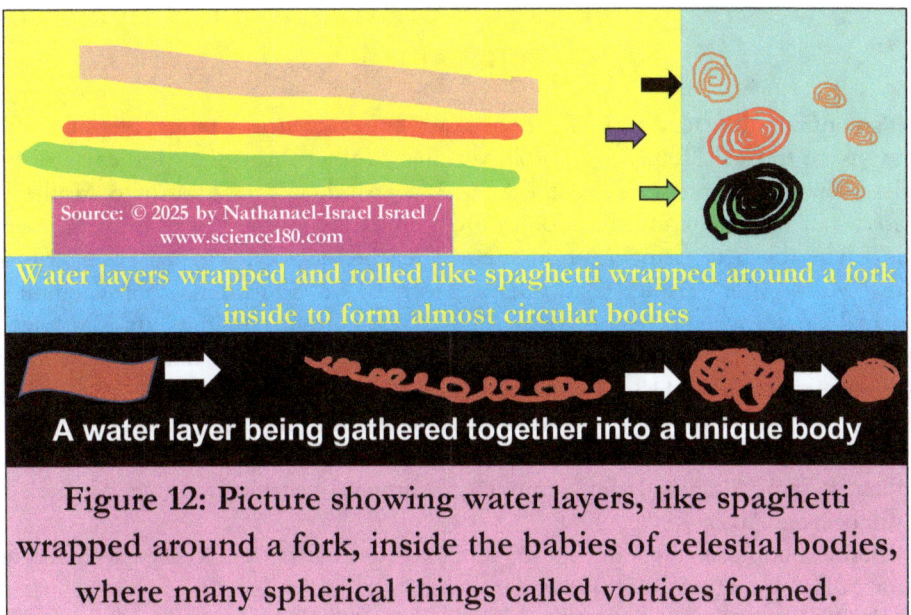

Source: © 2025 by Nathanael-Israel Israel / www.science180.com

Water layers wrapped and rolled like spaghetti wrapped around a fork inside to form almost circular bodies

A water layer being gathered together into a unique body

Figure 12: Picture showing water layers, like spaghetti wrapped around a fork, inside the babies of celestial bodies, where many spherical things called vortices formed.

9. How Mars, Jupiter, Saturn, Uranus, Neptune, and Pluto were formed

Let's continue the story and talk about how Jupiter, Saturn, Uranus, Neptune, and Pluto were formed. Remember, I told you that Mother 2 was the Mother of all the celestial bodies turning around the Sun. After Mother 2 gave birth to Mother 3 (Mother of the Earth and the Moon), it continued its journey away from the Baby Sun, giving birth to many asteroids until it reached a point when it gave birth to Baby Mars. After birthing Baby Mars, Mother 3 continued its journey until it reached a point when it birthed Baby Jupiter. The journey continued until Mother 3 reached another point where it gave birth to Baby Uranus. After Baby Uranus, Baby Neptune was born, and later Baby Pluto.

All of those babies grew up and became planets. For instance, Baby Jupiter grew up and became Jupiter. Baby Saturn grew up and became Saturn. Baby Uranus grew up and became Uranus. Baby Neptune grew up and became Neptune, while Baby Pluto became Pluto.

Before I continue the story, let me remind you of what we have said so far. After Baby Solar System was born, it grew up and became Mother Solar System. Then, Mother Solar System birthed two children: Baby 1, which grew up to become the Sun, and Baby 2, which grew up to become Mother 2, meaning the Mother of all the celestial bodies orbiting the Sun. We also learned that, as it was moving away from Baby Sun, Mother 2 birthed many children until it reached a certain point when it birthed Baby 3, which became Mother 3, the Mother of the Earth and the Moon. I hope you remember all that.

As Mother 2 was moving away from the Sun and giving birth to many children, it got older and smaller until it could no longer give birth to children anymore. After Mother 2 birthed all of its children, it died. Each of those children grew up, went through changes, and became adults. Some of those Adult children of Mother 2 gave birth to their own children. That is how some children of Mother 2 ended up giving birth to a planet orbited by (meaning moving around, which turned) some satellites. As a reminder, a satellite is a celestial body that orbits a planet, just like how the Moon orbits the Earth.

1 body that turns around a planet, just like how the Moon turns around the Earth.

Nathanael-Israel Israel: Known as the World's Most Accurate Universe-Origin Mathematician

10. Why does the Earth turn around the Sun while the Moon turns around the Earth?

As Daddy was saying this, I raised my hand and asked, "Why does the Earth turn around the Sun while the Moon turns around the Earth?

"Great question!" said Daddy. This is about how celestial bodies were formed in the universe. To explain this, Daddy talked to us about what is called a planetary system: a family of celestial bodies, including a planet and its satellites. In fact, each planetary system was a baby at one point. In other words, it was a baby planetary system that grew up to become a mother that birthed a Baby planet and Baby satellites.

When each Baby planet was born, it was positioned almost in the middle of what would become the planetary system and started turning around the Baby star. The way the Baby satellites were born caused them to start orbiting, meaning turning around, the planet in their planetary system. That is why, until today, all planets turn around a star and all satellites turn around a planet. Because the Sun is the star in the Solar System, all planets in the Solar System orbit the Sun. Likewise, all satellites turn around their planet. Hence, the Moon orbits the Earth. Jupiter, for instance, has more than 80 satellites, all of which orbit it. Do you understand? I hope so!

11. Why do some planets walk on their head, while others roll like a ball, and some are more bent than others

When Mother 2 was moving away from the Sun, it took a certain time before it birthed each of its babies. That is why the planets in the Solar System are not together but are separated by a huge distance. As those babies were being born, those who were born first moved faster than those who were born last. Some of those babies were holding hands as they were being born, and when their hands were separated, they were pushed into different directions, just as two people holding hands can be sent into two different directions when the hands are released. In the case of the celestial bodies when the hands were removed, some fell backwards. That is why some celestial bodies are walking on their heads, and others are tilted or oriented differently. Some of them, like Jupiter, are not flipped much because they are very heavy. When these babies were being born, they spun around or rotated; hence, in the end, all celestial bodies turn around all of the time. Some rotate very fast, while others are slow. For example, the Earth spins around completely once every 24 hours. Some planets take many months to complete a single rotation. During its spinning around, the Earth faces the Sun in the day, while in the night it does not face the Sun.

12. Why do planets have different sizes and colors?

Recalling what I have learned at school, I asked Daddy the following questions:
- Why are some planets gas, others solid, and some icy?
- Why do planets have different colors?

Planets have different colors because they are made of different chemicals. Mars usually looks red. Jupiter looks like an orange-and-white cloud. From space, the Earth looks blue.

Daddy told us that, just as human beings have different sizes, so also celestial bodies were born with different sizes. Some celestial bodies are very small, and others are very BIG. Jupiter and Saturn are the biggest planets orbiting the Sun. This is because their babies were very big.

All children of celestial bodies were smaller than their mothers. That is also why the water drops we obtained by throwing a ball of water in the air were smaller than the water we initially threw. Human beings give birth to children who can grow and become as big as, or even bigger than, their mother. But in the case of celestial bodies, the babies are always smaller than their mother. This is because a mother of celestial bodies had to break into many pieces before birthing its children.

13. Why are some planets solid, while others are gas or icy?

When Mother 2 was moving away from Baby Sun, its temperature decreased, which means its temperature went down, as it was moving away from Baby Sun.

Just as water put into a freezer can become ice, so also the children of Mother 2 that were born far away from the Sun were rich in ice. Some children born to Mother 2 are rich in gas, while others are solid, like the Earth. For example, Jupiter and Saturn are gas giants. Uranus and Neptune are filled with ice, while Mercury, Venus, Earth, Mars, and Pluto are very hard. It all boils down to how the Babies of Mother 2 were pressed down, compressed, or squeezed as they were being shaped. For instance, a slice of bread is very soft. But if a slice of bread is squeezed or compressed, it can become harder or more solid. The same thing happened when celestial bodies were being formed. Some babies of Mother 2 were squeezed to become solid like the Earth, while others were not that squeezed and became gas planets like Jupiter. In other words, some of the babies of Mother 2 were highly squeezed to birth a solid planet like the Earth, while others were less squeezed and birthed gigantic planets like Jupiter.

The temperature of the environment also played a role in what the babies' celestial bodies became. To illustrate or better explain what he was saying in a language that we children could understand, Daddy reminded us that the same water we drink when we eat can also become solid like ice, and also be gas like the steam when we cook food. In other words, water can be in the form of ice, liquid, or gas. If water is put in a very cold environment like a freezer, it freezes and becomes ice. If water is left at room temperature, it stays liquid. When water is boiled on the stove, it can evaporate, meaning it goes into the atmosphere like a gas that we can see in the form of water steam. Others were born in very cold environments and became rich in ice like Neptune.

14. Why do planets have different speeds, and why do those close to the Sun orbit the Sun faster than those far from the Sun?

Before I say something very important about this question, let me remind you that Mother 2 was the mother of all the celestial bodies orbiting around the Sun. As Mother 2 was moving away from Baby Sun, it was getting tired, and the babies it was giving birth to as it got older and older were moving more slowly. Part of this is because when Mother 2 was pregnant with its babies, they were stacked one on top of the other like pancakes and moved along a current like how a river flows. In fact, in a river, waters are stacked on top of each other, and they form water layers, like pancakes laid one on top of the other in a moving stream or in a flowing river. You may not know it, but it is very true that all the water in a river doesn't move at the same speed. In fact, in a river, the waters on top moved faster than those beneath them. In the end, the waters at the bottom move more slowly than any above them (see Figure 13).

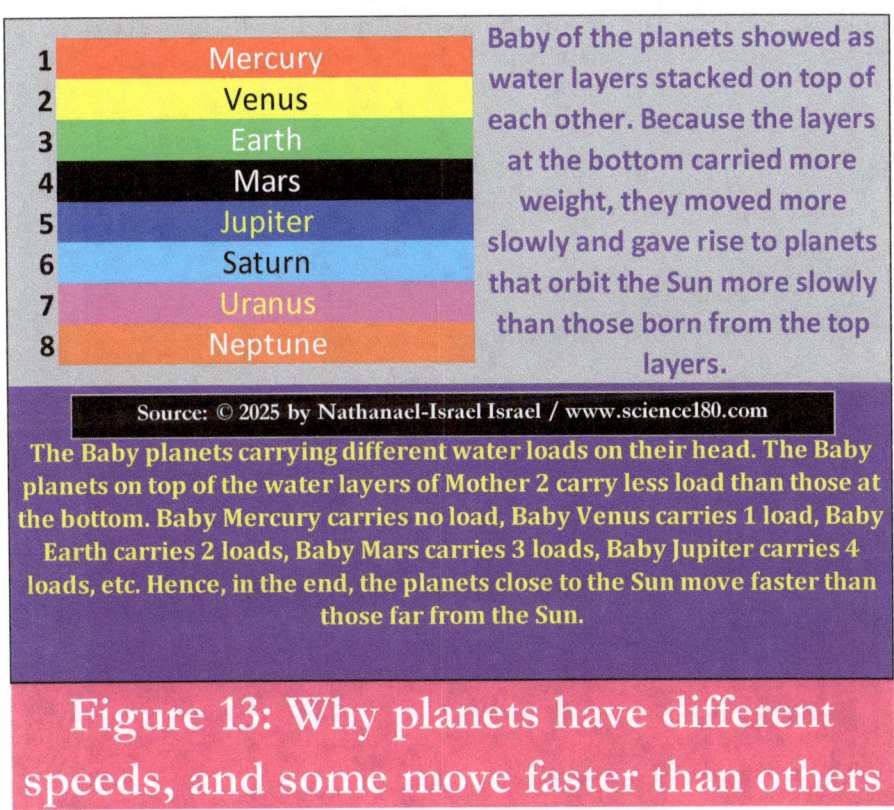

Baby of the planets showed as water layers stacked on top of each other. Because the layers at the bottom carried more weight, they moved more slowly and gave rise to planets that orbit the Sun more slowly than those born from the top layers.

Source: © 2025 by Nathanael-Israel Israel / www.science180.com

The Baby planets carrying different water loads on their head. The Baby planets on top of the water layers of Mother 2 carry less load than those at the bottom. Baby Mercury carries no load, Baby Venus carries 1 load, Baby Earth carries 2 loads, Baby Mars carries 3 loads, Baby Jupiter carries 4 loads, etc. Hence, in the end, the planets close to the Sun move faster than those far from the Sun.

Figure 13: Why planets have different speeds, and some move faster than others

Likewise, the first babies Mother 2 birthed were like the first pancakes or the first layers of water on top of the moving stream. Those babies moved faster. The pancakes on top pressed down on the pancakes below, and because the bottom ones were pressed, they carried the weight of those on top. In other words, the pancakes on the bottom moved slowly because they carried too much weight. That is why the first Baby Mother 2 gave birth moved faster than the last Baby. For instance, Mercury is the closest planet to the Sun, and it moves faster than any other planet in the Solar System. Venus, which was born after Mercury, moves more slowly than Mercury. Then the Earth, which was born after Venus, moves more slowly than Venus does. Mars was born after the Earth, and as you can imagine, Mars moves more slowly than Earth. Likewise, because Jupiter was born after Mars, Jupiter moves more slowly than Mars. Here, when I talk about movement, I mean how the planets orbit the Sun. The speed of the planets around the Sun is not about how big they are, but about how close or far they are from the Sun (Figure 13).

To wrap it up, the celestial bodies that are close to the Sun moved fast because they were born from the pancakes or water layers that were closer to the top of the water of Mother 2, but the celestial bodies that are farther away from the Sun move slower because they were born from the pancakes or water layers that were at the bottom of Mother 2. That is why the speed of the celestial bodies decreases from the closest body to the Sun all the way to the last body turning around the Sun.

15. Why do planets rotate?

At this point. Daddy asked us if we wanted to know *"Why do planets turn around?"* Joshua-Enoch replied *"No"* because he never knew that planets turn around, and that Daddy was teaching us was too much information for his head to understand, and he was ready for a break. But Joelle-Major and I told Daddy that we wanted to know why some planets turn around themselves. Then, Daddy asked my siblings if they knew what rotation meant.

Before he introduces a new topic to us, Daddy likes to know what we know about it, so he knows where to start his teaching. That is why Daddy likes to ask us questions. Only I knew about the rotation of planets.

To help explain what turning around or rotation is, Daddy took us to the dining room and pulled all of the chairs out from the circular dining room table. Daddy first made all of us walk around the table. As we were walking, he told us our movement at that time was like a celestial body orbiting the Sun, meaning a celestial body moving around the Sun. In other words, when a planet moves around the Sun, we say that it orbits the Sun.

Then, Daddy told us that celestial bodies do not move around the Sun like we walk around the dining room table. But the celestial bodies spin around themselves as they move around the Sun. To help us better understand how rotation works as planets orbit the Sun, Daddy told us to spin around while we went around the table. We started spinning in circles and orbiting the table. It was a cool experiment, and we started laughing. We quickly became very dizzy and had to stop, or we would have fallen. Therefore, Daddy told us to stop moving. He then told us that spinning around in circles is called turning around or rotation, while turning around the table is called revolution or orbital movement.

Then, Joelle-Major asked: *"How come we spun around for just a few minutes and were very dizzy and about to fall down, yet the planets have been spinning around themselves as they orbit the Sun for thousands of years, but they never get dizzy and fall down as we were about to fall down?"*

As she asked that question, I followed up and asked Daddy, *"Why do we get dizzy when we spin around?"* Daddy laughed and said that our questions are great and that we are very smart kids! He was also happy because he knew we were paying attention to what he was saying and that we were very curious.

Daddy then told us that when we turn around or spin for a long time, our bodies are shaken too much. Because that movement shakes our body and the brain in our head, it ends up affecting our whole body. The brain is something like a liquid containing some well-organized stuff, and when they are shaken, this stuff can be scrambled just as the yellow and white of an egg get messed up when they are scrambled.

Going back to Joelle-Major's question about why celestial bodies rotate like a tornado, Daddy said it all boils down to how they formed. He reminded us that the babies of the celestial bodies once moved like a stack of pancakes or the layers of water in a moving river. When water moves in a river, it is stacked on top of other water. As they move, the top layers flow faster than the bottom layers. As those layers of water in the baby planets were moving, they started collecting themselves in circles and rolling around just like how we can roll spaghetti around a fork. For example, a long spaghetti noodle can be rolled around a fork until it forms a solid thing around the fork. It is like a piece of yarn that you roll around into a ball. In the same manner, the water or liquid of the baby of the planet rolled around itself until it formed the planet, and the rolling continued in the form of the orbital movement and rotation, or the spinning around. That is why planets spin on their axes as they orbit the Sun. Daddy told us that in the books he wrote for adults, he had to better explain this very difficult subject called turbulence, something that is way beyond what children's minds could understand. Turbulence involves things that also explain how clouds are formed in the atmosphere and can produce heavy rain, like hurricanes or tornadoes. Now that we understand how the Sun and the planets were formed, let's move to other things.

16. How were the galaxies formed?

When Daddy asked us in the beginning of this book to write down our questions, one of the things that my sister Joelle-Major wanted to know was how galaxies were made. Daddy was a little surprised that she even knew what the word "galaxy" means. Although most children our age may have heard about the word "galaxy" and thought of it as a cool thing in the sky, Daddy was not sure if we really knew what a galaxy meant. Therefore, he started answering this big question by telling Joelle-Major: *"I know you heard about galaxies somewhere, but do you really know what a galaxy means?"*

All of us were sitting around the dining table, and Daddy was answering our questions and typing them at the same time. We started with Joshua-Enoch's questions, and Daddy answered them one by one in the order they were written down. Then, he answered the question of Joelle-Major next, and he finished with mine. As he was answering the questions, he told us if any of us did not understand anything, to stop him and ask. Obedient to his instructions, we stopped every time he said anything hard to understand or even when he said a word that was for adults. We asked many questions that he answered for us, but he did not include all of them in this book, for he said that if he were to include them all, it would be a huge book that people would not enjoy. Also, some questions were not about the books' topics. Before answering any question, he usually asked us what we knew about it. This gave us a chance to talk and speak about what was on our minds before Daddy improved it or corrected it.

Therefore, as I felt like Joelle-Major did not know what galaxies mean, although she was the one who asked that question, I quickly came to her rescue by saying that galaxies are made of many stars that are shaped in a special way, as if they were stuck together somehow.

"That is a pretty good answer," Daddy replied. Galaxies are made of many stars organized into groups. In other words, the stars in a galaxy are bound together like people in the same family.

As a reminder, the Solar System is a group of celestial bodies made of the Sun at the "center", and the planets and asteroids orbiting or turning around the Sun. Most stars belong to a specific galaxy. There are billions of galaxies in the universe, and most of them have not been discovered yet. The Sun and all the other celestial bodies in the Solar System belong to a galaxy called the Milky Way Galaxy. As soon as Daddy said the word "Milky Way," I asked him why they call our galaxy the Milky Way, when it is not made of milk.

"Very smart girl Josephine!" Daddy replied to me. Daddy always encouraged us to ask questions, and he was very happy when we asked difficult questions. Hearing Daddy call me smart, I smiled and looked at him. Then, Daddy said that our galaxy is called the Milky Way because it looks like milk or a stream of milk! In addition, Daddy told us that all the stars we see in the sky at night belong to the Milky Way galaxy. The Milky Way galaxy looks like a spiral. Then, Daddy asked us if we knew

what a spiral meant. I answered that a spiral is like spaghetti wrapped around a fork. Joshua-Enoch added that a spiral is like a snake wrapped around a leg. Because Daddy does not like snakes, he asked Joshua-Enoch to try again. This time, Joshua-Enoch said that a spiral is like ternary spinning around.

"*Good try,*" Daddy replied.

The universe contains many galaxies. Just as the Solar System was once a baby we called Baby Solar System, so were all the stars in the universe, along with their planets and asteroids. In the same manner, all the galaxies in the universe were once baby galaxies, which had to grow up to birth many babies who grew up and became stars orbited by planets and asteroids. In other words, all the galaxies in the universe were initially babies that grew up to give birth to all the stars, planets, asteroids, and other celestial bodies they contain. If you remember, I told you that the Sun is filled with fire, something like lava that is found in volcanoes, and also something called plasma. Similarly, all Baby galaxies were filled with Baby stars popping up here and there like popcorn or fireworks. That means that when galaxies were forming, the universe could have looked like a gigantic firework show.

In response to this statement, I said that Baby Universe could have been like a popcorn show. Everybody laughed at that illustration. Just as a firework pops up in the sky and births other fires, which also can pop, when the universe was being formed, huge Baby galaxies were popping up, giving birth to many stars everywhere. This was more than the July 4th fireworks that the Americans put up to celebrate their independence from the UK. Anyway, during the formation of the universe, no human being was formed yet; otherwise, very hot fireworks could have hurt, burned, or even killed them. At that time, no dinosaur, giraffe, or rhinoceros had been made yet. It was after the Earth was formed that animals, plants, and human beings were formed. I will get back to that later in this book.

Very soon, I will explain to you how all living things were made. Before that, let's do some STEAM to see how fast the universe was formed and who did that. I hope you understand that by the steam, I didn't mean the hot steam we use to cook food in our kitchen, but STEAM, which means Science, Technology, Engineering, Art, and Math. Even if you are not very good at science and math, we will help you understand it 100%.

Are you ready? Are you happy? Daddy asked.

With a loud voice, we all replied, "Yes." And he said, "Excellent." Let's go!

SECTION 3: POWERFUL MATH ABOUT HOW LONG IT TOOK TO FORM THE EARTH, THE MOON, AND THE SUN

17. Let's remember what we learned about the Solar System 's birth.

So far, we have been talking about how Baby Universe was born, but we have not talked yet about how long it took for it to be born. Daddy told us that when most women get pregnant, the baby stays inside the womb for about 9 months before being born.

"Why does a baby have to stay in mommy's belly for 9 months, while it can be taken out and grow?" I asked Daddy. He replied that all this is because it takes time for a baby to grow before it is ready for birth. After a baby is born, he or she will still need to grow before becoming a teenager, and later an adult.

"How long did Baby Universe take before birthing all the celestial bodies then?" I asked Daddy.

Before using science to address that issue, let's summarize what we have learned so far.

Daddy said that he will answer by first focusing on the Solar System, meaning the group or family of celestial bodies formed by the Sun and all the celestial bodies (including planets and asteroids) orbiting it. By the way, "orbiting" is a fancy way to say that a body is turning around another one, just as the planets in the Solar System turn around the Sun, or how the satellites turn around a planet.

Figure 14: Baby stars were popping up like popcorn in Baby Universe

Nathanael-Israel Israel: Author of "Reconciling Science and Creation Accurately"

We also learned that when Baby Universe was being born, many Baby stars were popping up here and there in space. It was during that process that Baby Solar System was born (see Figure 14). Then, Baby Solar System grew up to become Mother Solar System (see Figure 15) before giving birth to 2 babies, whom we called Baby 1 and Baby 2 (see Figure 16).

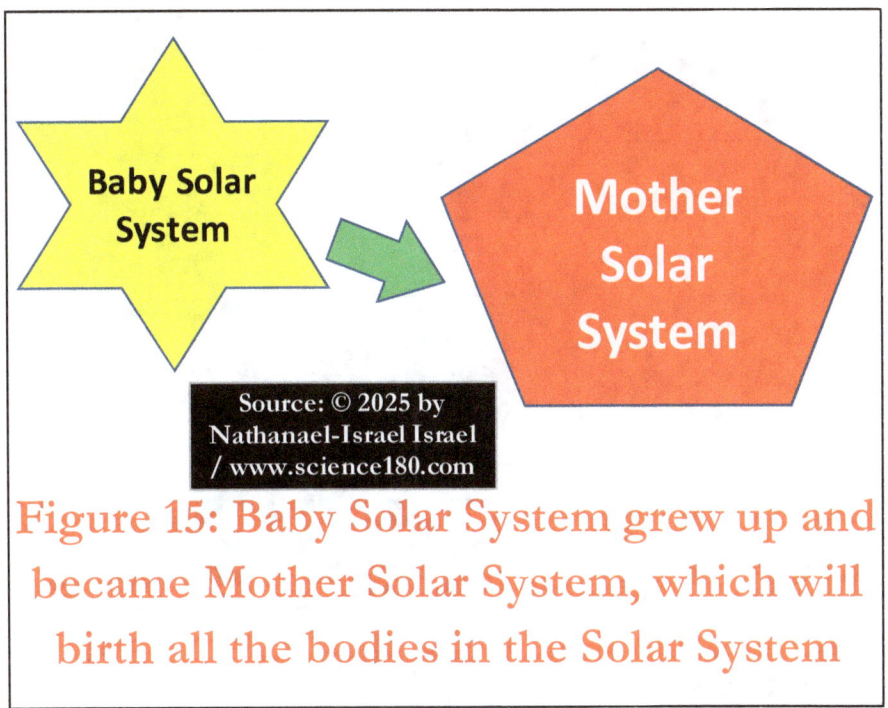

Source: © 2025 by Nathanael-Israel Israel / www.science180.com

Figure 15: Baby Solar System grew up and became Mother Solar System, which will birth all the bodies in the Solar System

Baby 1 was Baby Sun that grew up to become the Sun (see Figure 17). Baby 2 was the baby that grew up to become the Mother of all the celestial bodies orbiting the Sun. In other words, after Baby Sun was born, it was collected into the Adult Sun, while, in turn, Baby 2 grew up to become Mother 2, meaning the Mother of all the celestial bodies orbiting the Sun (see Figure 18).

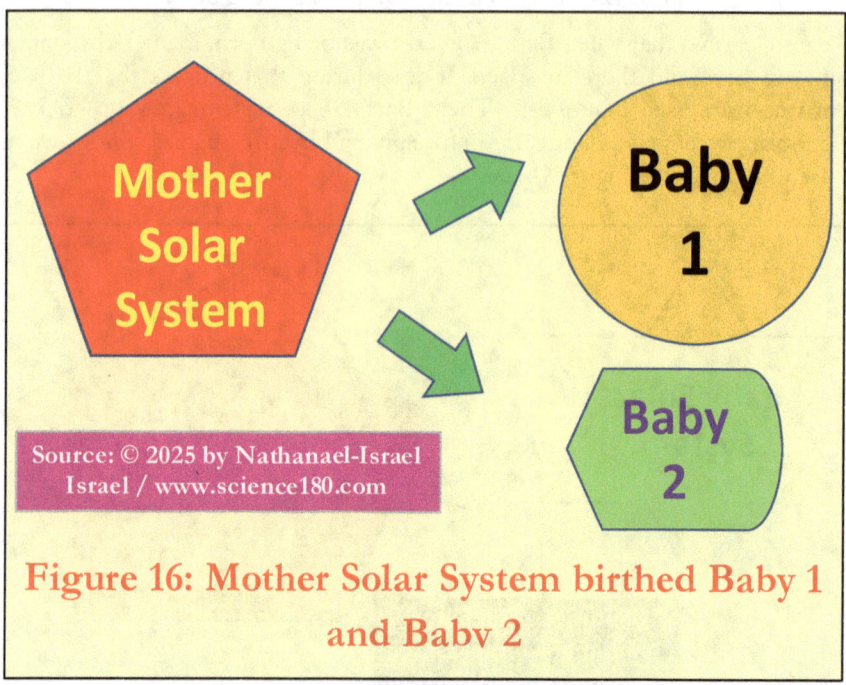

Source: © 2025 by Nathanael-Israel Israel / www.science180.com

Figure 16: Mother Solar System birthed Baby 1 and Baby 2

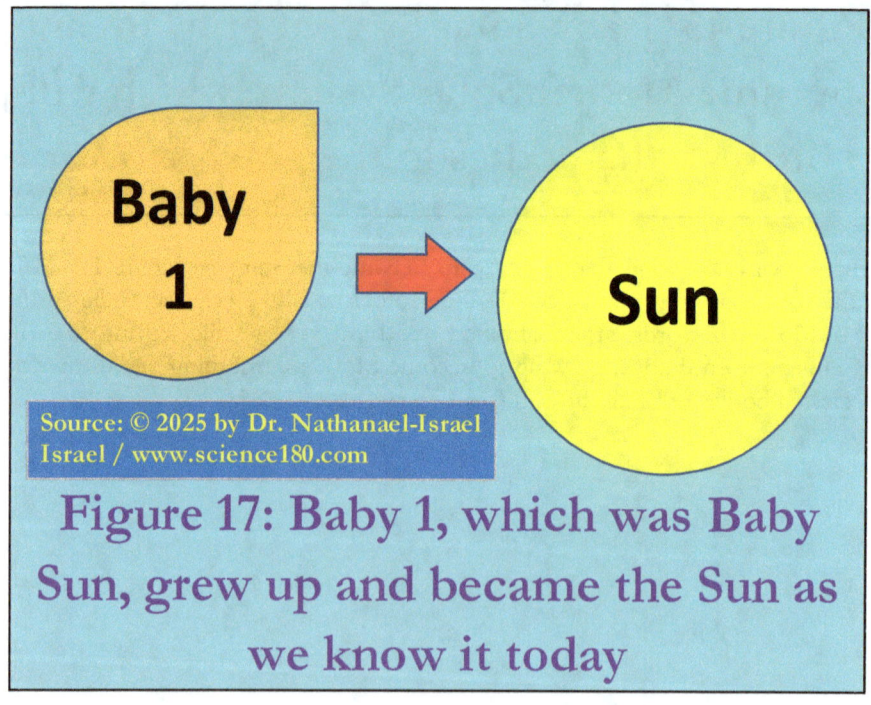

Source: © 2025 by Dr. Nathanael-Israel Israel / www.science180.com

Figure 17: Baby 1, which was Baby Sun, grew up and became the Sun as we know it today

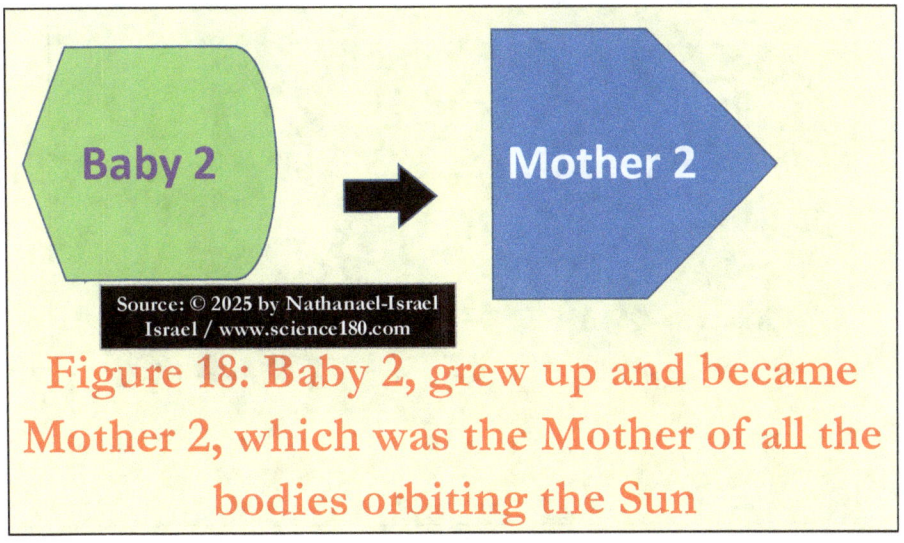

Figure 18: Baby 2, grew up and became Mother 2, which was the Mother of all the bodies orbiting the Sun

As Mother 2 was flowing like a river carrying many babies stacked one on top of the other like pancakes or water layers, each baby was born according to its position in the stack of pancakes. Some babies in the huge stack of Mother 2 became Baby planetary systems and grew up to become Mother planetary systems. By the way, a planetary system is a family of celestial bodies formed by a planet and its satellites. After a Baby planetary system formed and became a Mother planetary system, it then gave birth to a Baby planet and Baby satellites. Mother 2 also gave birth to many Baby asteroids between the Baby planets. The babies that were on top of the pancake stack or water layers were born first, and those that were at the bottom were born last. One of the very first babies Mother 2 gave birth to was Baby Mercury. After Baby Mercury was born, Mother 2 continued its journey away from Baby Sun until it reached a certain point when it birthed Baby 3 (see Figure 19), which quickly grew up and became Mother 3, meaning the Mother of the Earth and the Moon (see Figure 20).

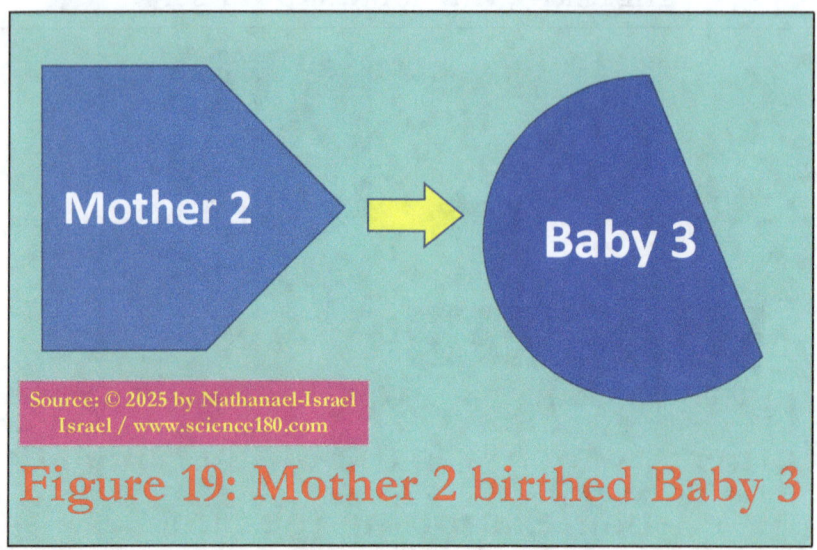

Source: © 2025 by Nathanael-Israel
Israel / www.science180.com

Figure 19: Mother 2 birthed Baby 3

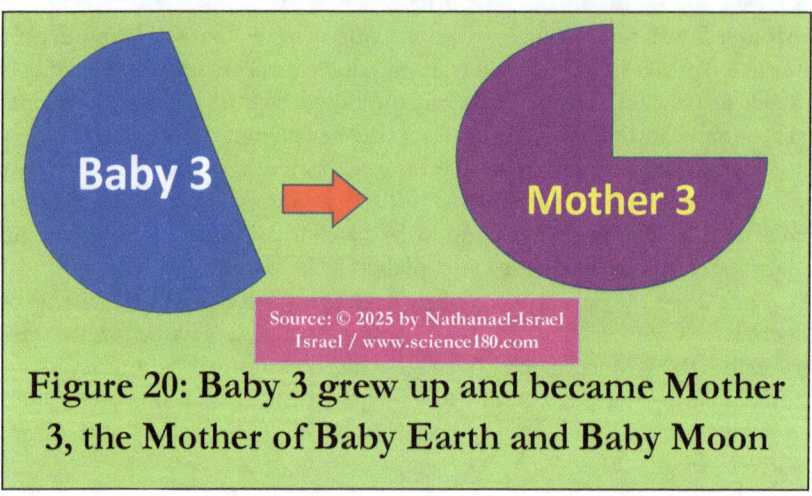

Source: © 2025 by Nathanael-Israel
Israel / www.science180.com

Figure 20: Baby 3 grew up and became Mother 3, the Mother of Baby Earth and Baby Moon

Then, the Mother of the Earth and the Moon fast birthed Baby Earth and Baby Moon (see Figure 21). As you can see in Figures 22 and 23, after some changes to their bodies, Baby Earth became the Earth and Baby Moon became the Moon.

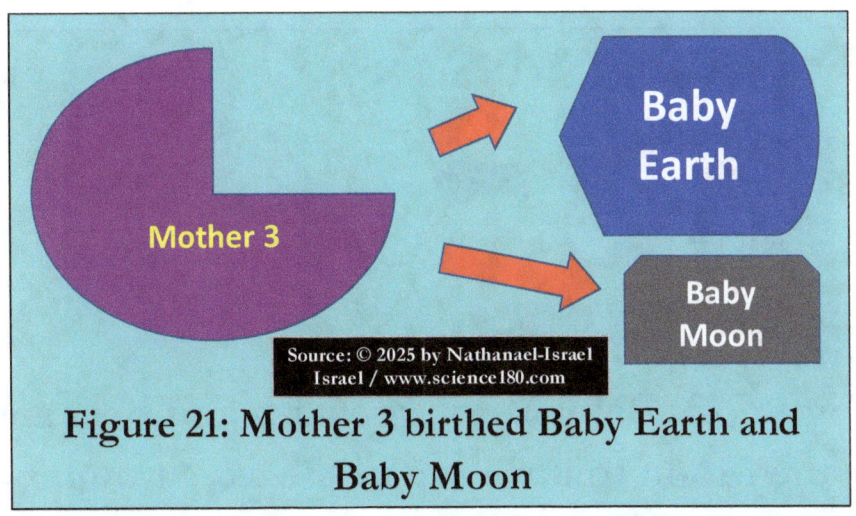

Source: © 2025 by Nathanael-Israel
Israel / www.science180.com

Figure 21: Mother 3 birthed Baby Earth and Baby Moon

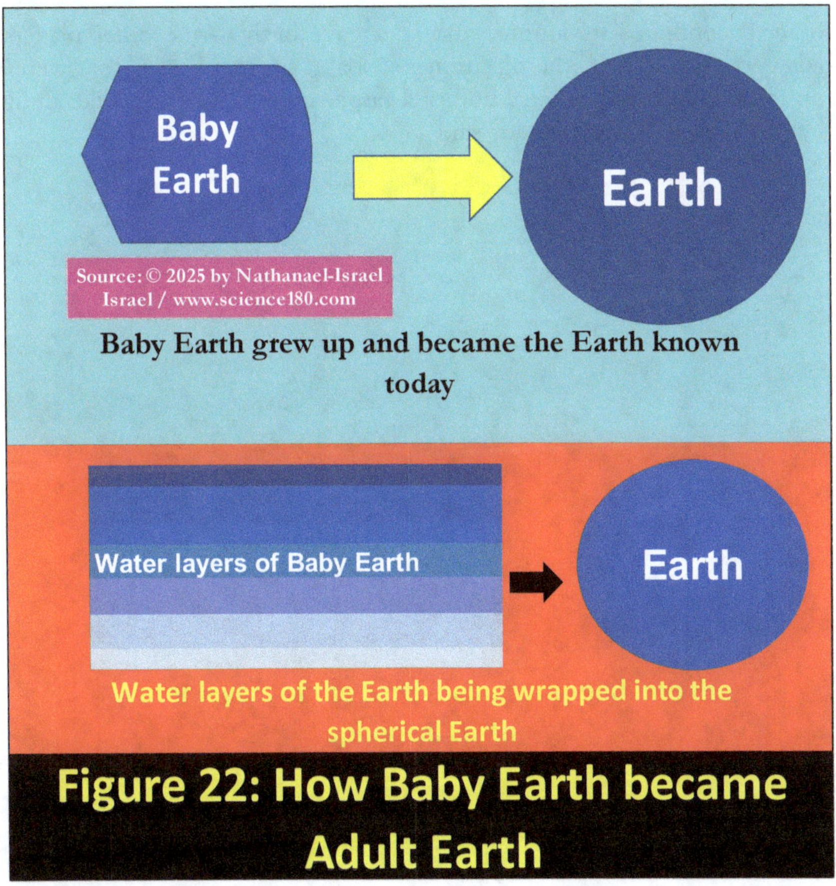

Source: © 2025 by Nathanael-Israel
Israel / www.science180.com

Baby Earth grew up and became the Earth known today

Water layers of Baby Earth

Earth

Water layers of the Earth being wrapped into the spherical Earth

Figure 22: How Baby Earth became Adult Earth

Science180: The Premier Organization that Scientifically Decoded the Origin
of the Universe, Life, and Chemicals Accurately

Figure 23: Baby Moon grew up and became the Moon that we see in the sky at night

Mother 2 continued its journey and later gave birth to the other planets and asteroids beyond Earth. In the meantime, all Baby celestial bodies that were born grew up to become Adult celestial bodies. I hope you remember and like all of this. *"Yes,"* we all replied. *"Good"*, Daddy said.

18. How can we use STEAM (Science, Technology, Engineering, Art, and Math) to calculate the time it took for the Earth, the Moon, and the Sun to be formed?

To demonstrate means to prove or to show how that thing happened. For example, demonstrating how long the Earth took to form means showing how long it took before it was formed. We will also demonstrate how long it took for the Moon and the Sun to be formed. Before we do that, I need to explain two important words: distance and speed. People in the US like to measure distance in miles, but people in Africa and Europe prefer to use kilometers. By the way, one mile is about 1.61 kilometers. Let's consider an example.

Because my family's house is close to the elementary school my brother, sister, and I attend (the school we go to), we walk every morning to get to class. From our home to the school is about half a mile. That half a mile is called a distance. In other words, a distance is the length or the amount of space separating two things or people. The distance we walked every morning to go to school is the length separating our home and our school.

To get to the school, we usually walk at a certain pace that works for all of us. Because we have shorter legs than Daddy, we cannot walk as fast as he does. Therefore, he slows down as much as possible so we can all catch up with him without having to run. What a great Dad I have!

We usually take about 10 minutes to walk the half mile separating our home and our school. Because we can walk half a mile in 10 minutes, it means that we can walk a whole mile in about 20 minutes. The math I did to know that we can walk one mile in 20 minutes is called "multiplication." I multiplied 10 minutes by 2 to get 20 minutes, and I also multiplied half a mile by 2 to get one mile. I hope you understand; if not, let me put it in a real scientific way: $10 \times 2 = 20$ and $\frac{1}{2} \times 2 = 1$. By the way, $\frac{1}{2}$ is what scientists write as 0.5.

To speak like a mathematician (meaning someone who is good at math), we will say that we can walk about 1 mile in 20 minutes. Because there are 60 minutes in one hour, if we walk 1 mile every 20 minutes, we can then walk about 3 miles in 1 whole hour, provided we don't stop and take a break. To say that we can walk about 3 miles per hour is to say that our speed is 3 miles per hour, written as 3 miles/hour. In other words, speed is a way to say how much distance you can cover within a certain amount of time. Some people can walk faster; others can run faster. Olympians, athletes who compete at the Olympics, are usually the fastest and set records.

To calculate how long it takes to walk, run, or fly over a certain distance at a certain speed, the math that is usually done is to divide the distance by the speed. For example, let's calculate how long it will take to walk 6 miles at a speed of 3 miles per hour. Here, the distance is 6 miles and the speed is 3 miles per hour. Dividing the distance by the speed gives the time it would take to walk 6 miles at 3 miles per

Science180: The Premier Organization that Scientifically Decoded the Origin of the Universe, Life, and Chemicals Accurately

hour: $6 \div 3 = 2$. In other words, it will take 2 hours to walk 6 miles at a speed of 3 miles per hour.

"*Why are we saying all this stuff about distance and speed, while we were supposed to be talking about the Earth, the Moon, and the Sun?*" Joshua-Enoch asked.

"*This is because Baby Earth, Baby Moon, and Baby Sun have also traveled a certain distance at a certain speed before being formed,*" Daddy replied. To figure out how long it took for them to be formed, we need to consider the distance that their babies traveled and at what speed they moved. This is because the Mothers of the celestial bodies traveled from a certain point to another point, meaning over a certain distance, before reaching a position where they were finally wrapped around like spaghetti wrapped around a fork. I hope you remember that we said the Baby celestial bodies were like water layers or spaghetti layers, collected or put together like spaghetti wrapped around a fork.

On top of the time it took for the Mother celestial body to travel the distance I just mentioned, it also took some time for their water layers, or spaghetti layers, or pancake layers to be wrapped around. In the end, the total amount of time it took for the celestial bodies to be formed is the addition of the time their mother traveled and the time it took to wrap their layers of water or whatever materials their babies contained into a round body, looking like a sphere or like spaghetti wrapped around a fork. Now, let's use this math to calculate how long it took for the Earth, the Moon, and the Sun to be formed. I hope you have been enjoying the pretty, artistic pictures we spent a lot of time designing to illustrate the difficult problems we are solving in this book. If yes, let's continue.

Nathanael-Israel Israel: Author of "Reconciling Science and Creation Accurately"

19. How long did it take for the Earth to be formed?

Using the speed of Mother 2 and the distance separating the Sun and the Earth, my Daddy, Dr. Nathanael-Israel Israel, was the first person in history to figure out how long it took before Baby Earth was born. By dividing the distance separating the Sun and Earth by the speed at which Mother 2 traveled, Daddy calculated how long it took before Mother 2 moved from the position of Baby Sun to about the position where Mother 3 (also called the Mother of Baby Earth and Baby Moon) was born.

Many people across the globe have studied the Earth and the Sun to determine how fast they move, what their size is, and how much distance separates them. For instance, NASA (National Aeronautics and Space Administration) is a big place where astronauts work in the US. As you can see in Figure 24, NASA has shown that the distance between the Sun and the Earth is about 93 million miles (149.6 million kilometers)! Wow! That's huge.

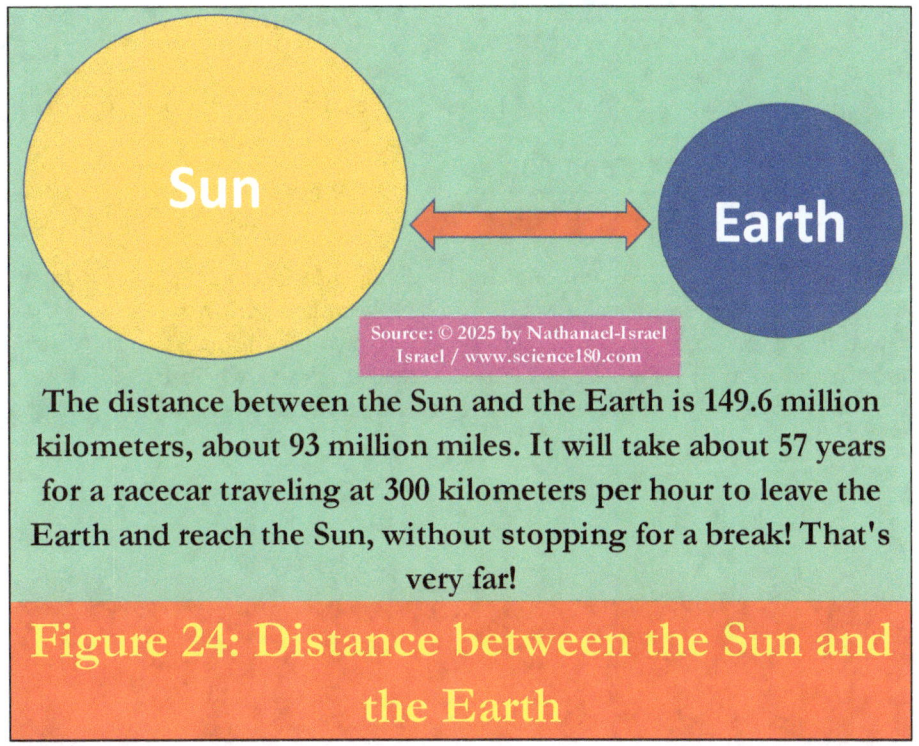

Source: © 2025 by Nathanael-Israel Israel / www.science180.com

The distance between the Sun and the Earth is 149.6 million kilometers, about 93 million miles. It will take about 57 years for a racecar traveling at 300 kilometers per hour to leave the Earth and reach the Sun, without stopping for a break! That's very far!

Figure 24: Distance between the Sun and the Earth

Based on research using NASA-collected data, Daddy (aka Nathanael-Israel Israel) determined that Mother 2's speed was about 617.6 kilometers per second. That speed of 617.6 kilometers per second is what NASA called "escape velocity" of the Sun. Because Baby Earth was formed quickly after Mother 3 was born, my

Daddy proved for the first time in history that, by dividing the distance separating the Sun and the Earth by the speed that Mother 2 traveled, he discovered how long it took before Baby Earth arrived at the position of Earth since the moment Mother 2 started moving away from Baby Sun.

I know how to divide 4 by 2 to get 2. But I don't know how to divide the huge distance between the Sun and the Earth (149.6 million kilometers) by the speed of Mother 2 (617.6 kilometers per second) to obtain the duration I just mentioned. Therefore, to help me, Daddy took his machine called a calculator and plugged the number in to get the result: 149.6 million kilometers divided by 617.6 kilometers per second = 67.29 hours. One more time, the math I just showed you was discovered by my Daddy, and I am very proud of him.

To write down this math in a scientific way, I will first tell you that 149.6 million kilometers is written like 149,600,000 km. Therefore, 149.6 million kilometers divided by 617.6 kilometers per second is scientifically written like:

$$\frac{149,600,000 \text{ km}}{617.6 \text{ km/s}} = 67.29 \text{ hours}$$

In other words, the time that Mother 2 traveled before birthing Baby 3 is:

$$\frac{149,600,000 \text{ km}}{617.6 \text{ km/s}} = 67.29 \text{ hours}$$

Because there are 24 hours in one day, by dividing 67.29 hours by 24, Daddy got 2.8 days, which is more than 2 days, but not quite 3 days yet. In other words, as I showed in Figure 25, it took 67.29 hours or 2.8 days for Mother 2 to travel from about the position of Baby Sun to the position of the Earth where Baby Earth was born. But Baby Earth was not the Adult Earth we know today.

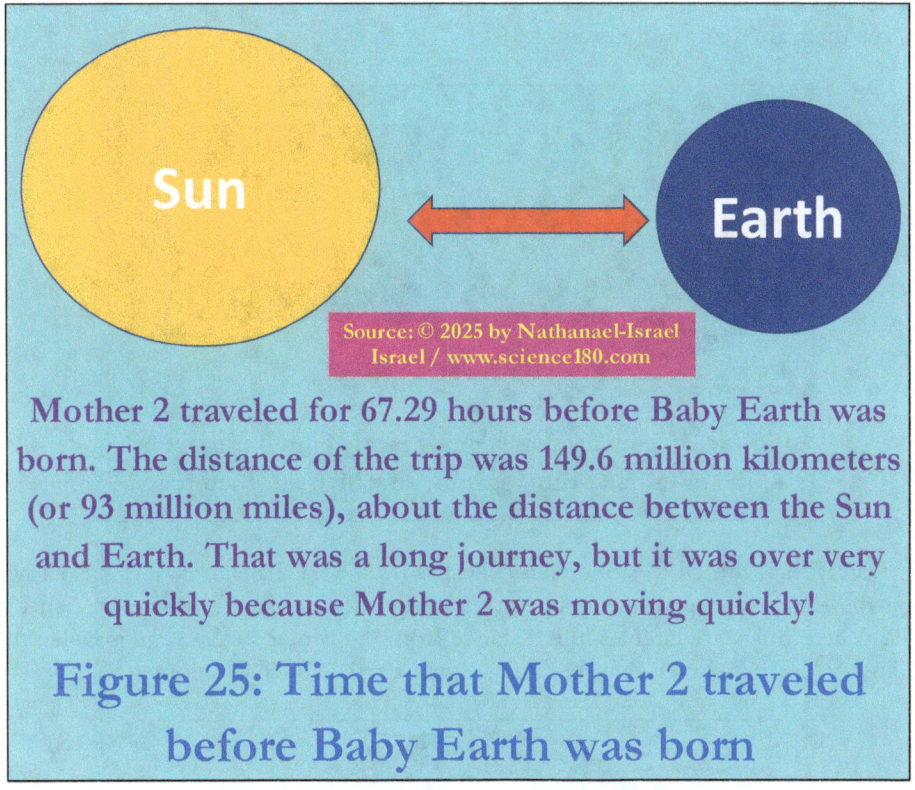

Mother 2 traveled for 67.29 hours before Baby Earth was born. The distance of the trip was 149.6 million kilometers (or 93 million miles), about the distance between the Sun and Earth. That was a long journey, but it was over very quickly because Mother 2 was moving quickly!

Figure 25: Time that Mother 2 traveled before Baby Earth was born

In fact, when Baby Earth was born, it was like water or spaghetti organized in layers or sheets flowing like a river that needed to be rolled around a big fork. My sister Joelle-Major went on to ask Daddy: *"How big were those sheets or layers of water looking like spaghetti that were in Baby Earth?"* *"Great question,"* Daddy replied. Before Daddy answered, I asked him another follow-up question: *"Why was Baby Earth wrapped around like spaghetti, but the dirt or soil on Earth is not sweet like the spaghetti we eat in pasta and rice?"*

"What a fantastic question!" Daddy said. To answer, he first said that when he compared the water layers of Baby Earth to spaghetti, he did not mean that Baby Earth was really spaghetti or noodles. But he meant that the water layers in Baby Earth contained things that were wrapped around like spaghetti or organized in layers like pancakes, one on top of the other. That is why the Adult Earth does not have spaghetti today. However, if we dig deep into the Earth, we will come across soil layers containing spiral structures organized as spaghetti rolled around a fork. For instance, when people dig a well to reach water underground, they discover many layers of soil with different colors and chemicals (see Figure 26). Because some of those spiral things are very small, you may need a microscope to zoom in on them before you can see some of them. Some of those spiral things turned out

to be rocks, minerals, atoms, etc. (by the way, "etc." is read as "etcetera," and it means there are many more examples).

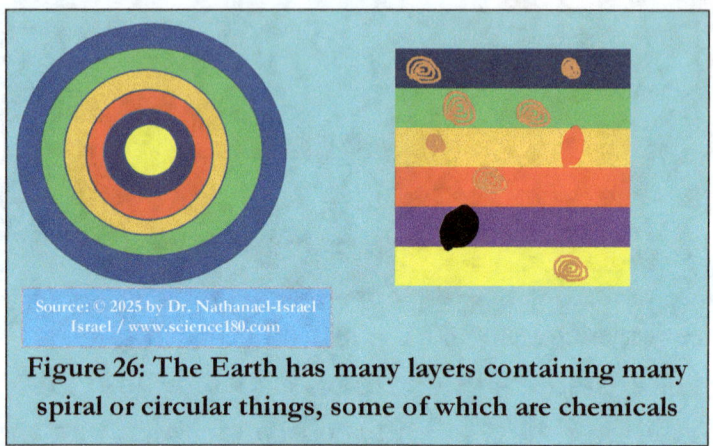

Source: © 2025 by Dr. Nathanael-Israel Israel / www.science180.com

Figure 26: The Earth has many layers containing many spiral or circular things, some of which are chemicals

Daddy then turned to some data collected by NASA. In fact, NASA has shown that the Earth is shaped like a sphere, meaning it looks like an orange or a cheese ball. When things are circular, the distance from the center to the edge is called the radius. NASA has shown that the radius of the Earth is 6378.14 kilometers.

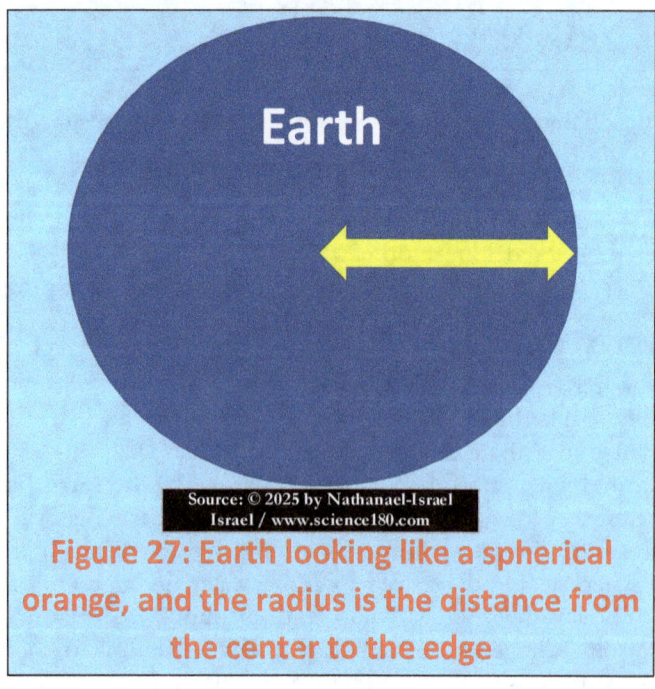

Source: © 2025 by Nathanael-Israel Israel / www.science180.com

Figure 27: Earth looking like a spherical orange, and the radius is the distance from the center to the edge

Nathanael-Israel Israel: Author of "Reconciling Science and Creation Accurately"

SECTION 3: POWERFUL MATH ABOUT HOW LONG IT TOOK TO FORM THE EARTH, THE MOON, AND THE SUN

Using the radius of the Earth, my Daddy has shown that the length of the sheets or layers of water or spaghetti in Baby Earth was about the distance around the perimeter of the Earth. That distance all the way around is called the circumference (see Figure 28).

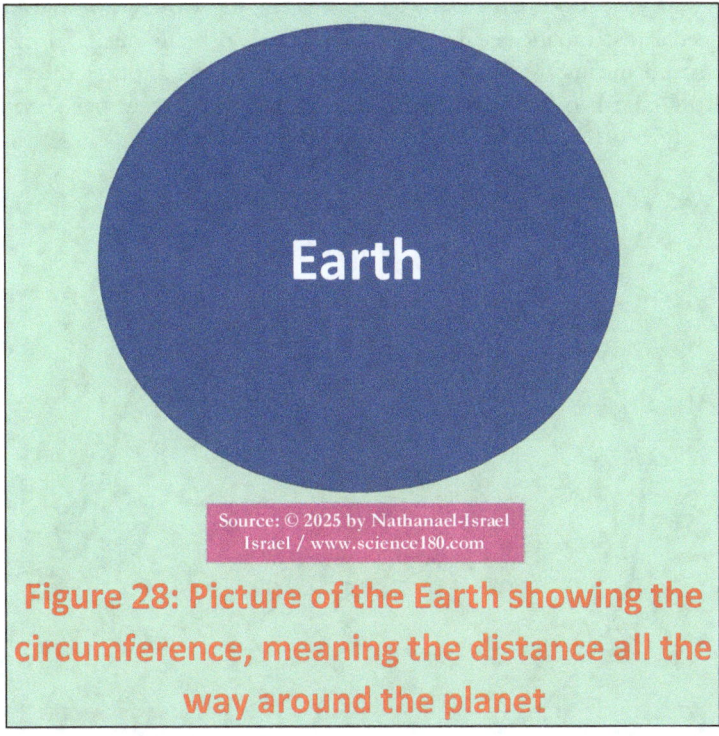

Source: © 2025 by Nathanael-Israel Israel / www.science180.com

Figure 28: Picture of the Earth showing the circumference, meaning the distance all the way around the planet

If you cannot pronounce that word, don't worry about it; I will do my best to ensure you understand what comes next. Using some math, Daddy calculated the distance to be about 40,054 km. In other words, the water layers in Baby Earth were about 40,054 km. Those water sheets were later wrapped around like 40,054 km of spaghetti rolled around a fork.

Using the math that I did in the story I told you concerning how we walk to school every morning, I hope you remember that time can be calculated by dividing a distance by a speed:

$$\text{Time} = \frac{\text{Distance traveled}}{\text{Speed of the travel}}$$

The math I just showed about time is called a formula. But don't get me wrong: by formula, I did not mean the formula that a mother gives to her baby, like milk, but by formula, I meant a way to write an equation of something. Welcome to our

49

school of STEAM!

Therefore, before calculating how long it took to wrap those water layers, I need to show you the speed at which they were wrapped. In fact, after many years of research, my Daddy showed that the speed at which the water layers in Baby Earth were wrapped around was about the same as the speed at which the Earth moved around the Sun. For those who want to learn some big words, I would like to note that the speed I just mentioned is called the Earth's orbital speed. In other words, the orbital speed means the speed at which a body orbits another one. NASA has shown that the Earth orbits the Sun at about 29.78 kilometers per second (Figure 29).

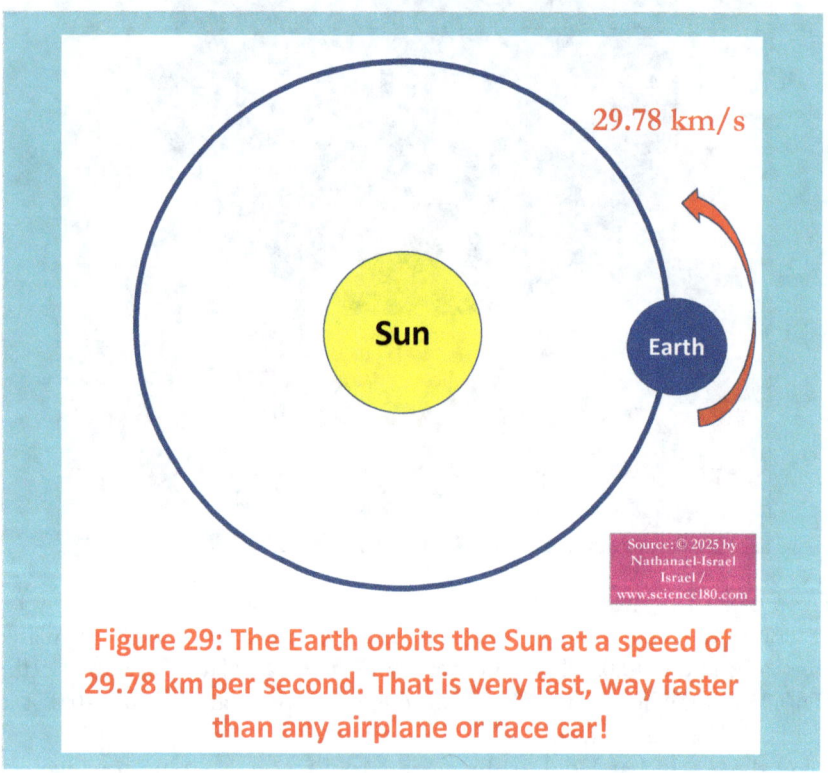

Figure 29: The Earth orbits the Sun at a speed of 29.78 km per second. That is very fast, way faster than any airplane or race car!

Now that we know the distance or length of the water layers or sheets in Baby Earth and also the speed at which they were rolled, we can calculate how long it took for Baby Earth to roll all its water layers around to become Adult Earth. My Daddy was the first person in history to show that by dividing the circumference of the Earth (meaning the distance all around) by the orbital speed (meaning the speed at which the Earth orbits or moves around the Sun), we can know how long it took for Baby Earth to become Adult Earth.

Nathanael-Israel Israel: Author of "Reconciling Science and Creation Accurately"

Time to wrap Baby Earth's water layers =
Circumference of the Earth /Orbital speed of the Earth

As a reminder, I told you a while ago that the circumference (meaning the distance all around the Earth) is 40,054 km and the orbital speed (which is the speed of the rolling) is about 29.78 kilometers per second. By dividing 40,054 km by 29.78 km/s, Daddy got 22.41 minutes. Let's put this math in a nice way that scientists will like:

$$\frac{40,054 \text{ km}}{29.7 \text{ km/s}} = 22.41 \text{ minutes}$$

In other words, after Baby Earth was born, it took just 22.41 minutes for its water layers or water sheet that was flowing like a river to be collected into the Adult Earth.

Then, Daddy went on to show us how long it took for the Earth to be fully formed. This amount of time includes 2 things:

- the time it took for Mother 2 to move from about the position of Baby Sun to the position where Baby Earth was born, and
- the time it took for Baby Earth to collect its water layers into a spherical body (looking like an orange) to become Adult Earth.

Remember, I showed you a while ago that after Baby 2 left Baby 1 (meaning Baby Sun), it took 67.29 hours for Baby Earth to be born. By the way, Baby 2 was the Baby that became Mother 2, which was the Mother of all the celestial bodies orbiting the Sun. Daddy demonstrated that, after Baby Earth was born, like water sheets or layers containing long things like spaghetti or noodles, it took about 22.41 minutes to wrap around all its waters to become the Adult Earth we know today. Therefore, according to my Daddy, Dr. Nathanael-Israel Israel, the total time it took for Baby Earth to form and become Adult Earth is 67.29 hours + 22.41 minutes, which equals about 67.66 hours. Because 1 day equals 24 hours, to find how many days there are in 67.66 hours, we divide 67.66 by 24, and we get 2.82 days. Let's put this like a formula:

67.29 hours + 22.41 minutes = 67.66 hours

To convert these hours into days, we divided them by 24:

$$\frac{67.66 \text{ hours}}{24 \text{ hours/day}} = 2.82 \text{ days}$$

By the way, 2.82 days means it wasn't quite the end of the 3rd day yet, but more

**Science180: The Premier Organization that Scientifically Decoded the Origin
of the Universe, Life, and Chemicals Accurately**

than 2 days had already passed. In other words, the Earth was born on the 3rd day of creation. In other words, since the beginning of the formation of the Solar System or the universe, it took about 67.29 hours for the Earth to be fully formed. And that was on the third day of creation. All the cool things I am teaching you about how the Universe was formed were discovered by my Daddy, and he taught me those things in a way children my age can understand. Let's recap using some artistic pictures (Figure 30 and Figure 31). We will also use our technology and engineering skills to fix those images.

Baby Earth was like water layers that were rolled like spaghetti around a fork. The water layers were as long as the circumference (perimeter around) of the Earth (which is 40,054 km). The rolling around took 22.41 minutes. In other words, it took 22.41 minutes for the long "noodles" of Baby Earth to become circular "noodles" or the spherical Earth.

After all the water layers were wrapped around, the inside of the Earth looked like layers stacked on top of each other. That is why, when people dig well, they find soil layers.

The Earth looks spherical, but people don't know that its layers are due to how it was formed

Source: © 2025 by Nathanael-Israel Israel / www.science180.com

Figure 30: Water layers of Baby Earth were rolled like spaghetti noodles around a fork

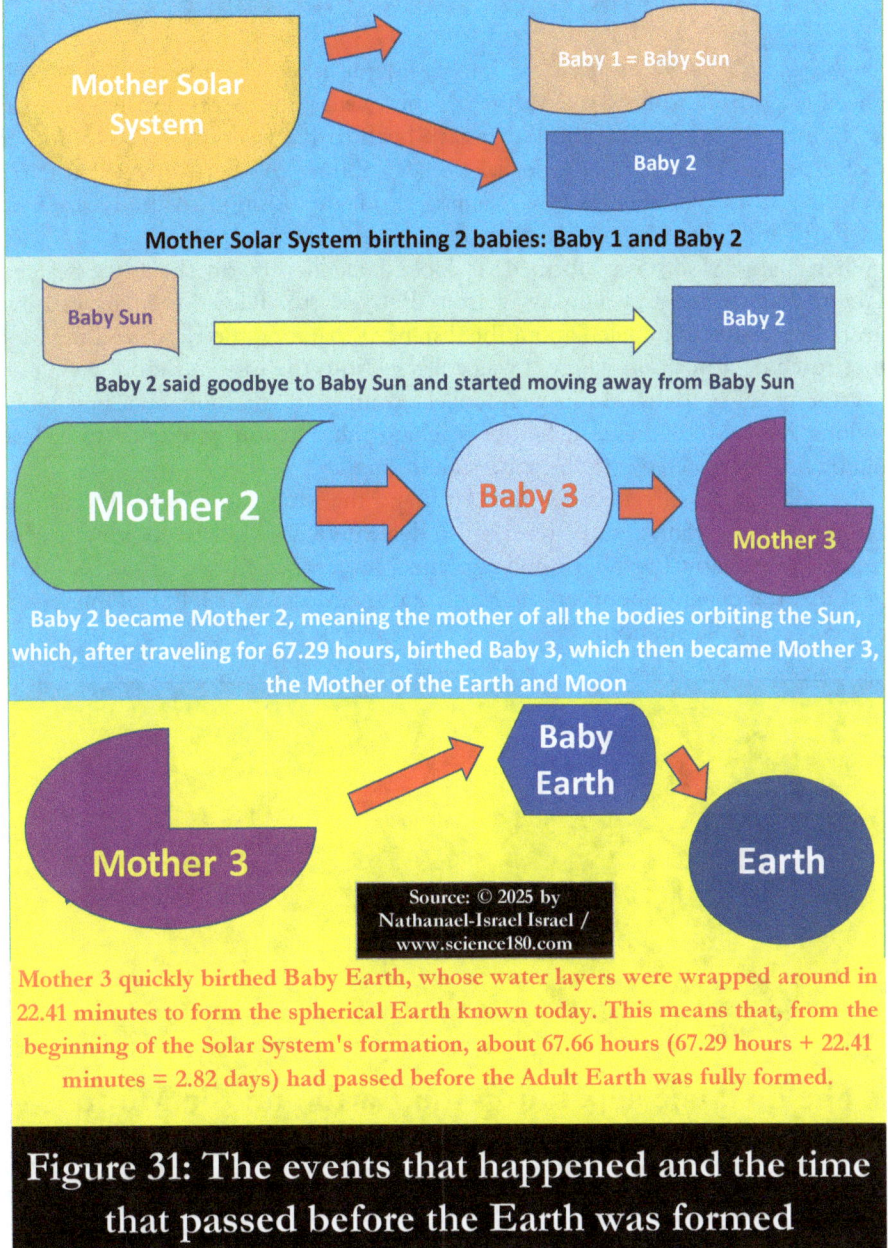

Mother Solar System

Baby 1 = Baby Sun

Baby 2

Mother Solar System birthing 2 babies: Baby 1 and Baby 2

Baby Sun

Baby 2

Baby 2 said goodbye to Baby Sun and started moving away from Baby Sun

Mother 2

Baby 3

Mother 3

Baby 2 became Mother 2, meaning the mother of all the bodies orbiting the Sun, which, after traveling for 67.29 hours, birthed Baby 3, which then became Mother 3, the Mother of the Earth and Moon

Baby Earth

Mother 3

Earth

Source: © 2025 by
Nathanael-Israel Israel /
www.science180.com

Mother 3 quickly birthed Baby Earth, whose water layers were wrapped around in 22.41 minutes to form the spherical Earth known today. This means that, from the beginning of the Solar System's formation, about 67.66 hours (67.29 hours + 22.41 minutes = 2.82 days) had passed before the Adult Earth was fully formed.

Figure 31: The events that happened and the time that passed before the Earth was formed

Now that we are done with the time it took for the Earth to be formed, let's turn to the Moon.

20. How long did it take for the Moon to be formed?

"*How long did it take to form the Moon*"? Joelle-Major asked. To answer that question, we need to go back to how the Mother of the Earth and the Moon were born, and how, in turn, the Mother of the Earth gave birth to Baby Moon. In fact, Mother 2 (which was the Mother of all celestial bodies orbiting the Sun) traveled for 67.29 hours away from Baby Sun before reaching about the position of the Earth, where Baby Earth and Baby Moon were formed.

When Baby Moon was formed, it looked like layers or sheets of water or spaghetti that started traveling away from Baby Earth. Baby Moon moved away from Baby Earth and traveled about the distance separating the Earth and the Moon before reaching a position where it was collected into the Moon. Before saying how the water layers of Baby Moon were collected into Adult Moon, let's first look at how long Baby Moon traveled before reaching the position where its water layers could be finally collected into the spherical Moon.

By using the distance between the Earth and the Moon and Baby Moon's travel speed, Daddy has done a lot of research to determine how long it took Baby Moon to travel from Baby Earth's position to the Moon's current position. NASA has shown that the distance between the Earth and the Moon is 384,400 kilometers. See Figure 32 for the illustration.

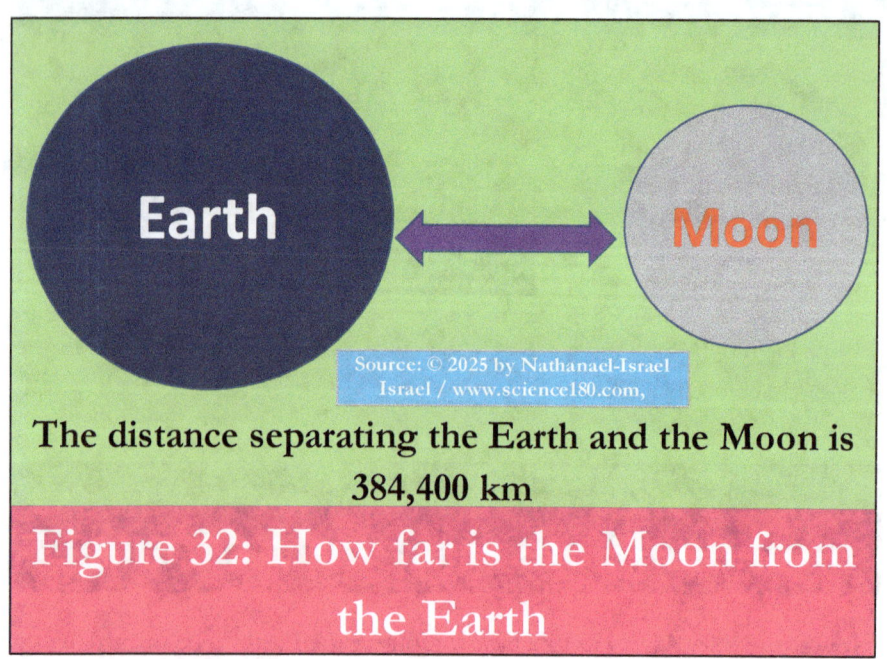

The distance separating the Earth and the Moon is 384,400 km

Figure 32: How far is the Moon from the Earth

Using data collected by NASA on the movement of celestial bodies, my Daddy has shown, for the first time in history, that the speed at which Baby Moon traveled

SECTION 3: POWERFUL MATH ABOUT HOW LONG IT TOOK TO FORM THE EARTH, THE MOON, AND THE SUN

away from Baby Earth was about 11.2 kilometers per second. That speed of 11.2 kilometers per second is called Earth's escape velocity. By the way, the verb "escape" means to leave, run away, or flee from something or someone. For many centuries and decades (a century means 100 years), scientists were aware of escape velocity, but they never knew that Baby Moon escaped Baby Earth at a speed close to Earth's escape velocity. Likewise, for more than 300 years after the work of the great scientist Isaac Newton, scientists did not know that Mother 2 escaped Baby Sun at a speed close to the Sun's escape velocity. My Daddy, Dr. Nathanael-Israel Israel, was the first human being to make such a great discovery. He figured it out after spending about 10 years of research on the origin of the celestial bodies. He was working on this even before any of us, his children, were born.

Therefore, Baby Moon traveled 384,400 kilometers at a speed of 11.2 kilometers per second before reaching the position of the Moon. By dividing the distance traveled by the Moon by the speed of travel, we can figure out how long the journey of Baby Moon took.

Because the distance and the speed of the Moon are too huge, I was not able to do that division by myself. Because my daddy is very smart, he took the calculator again and plugged the number in. When I said Daddy plugged the number into the calculator, I did not mean he plugged it inside the calculator like how we plug a charger into the hole, or an electric car to a battery, but I meant that Daddy used his fingers to enter the number into his calculator:

384,400 kilometers divided by 11.2 kilometers per second, and the answer is 9.53 hours

Written like a formula, what I just said is:

$$\frac{384,400 \text{ km}}{11.2 \text{ km/s}} = 9.53 \text{ hours}$$

I hope you are liking this. As you can see in Figure 33, these 9.53 hours mean that after Baby Moon was formed and left Baby Earth, it took about 9.53 hours before it reached the position of the Moon we know today. By the way, 9.53 hours equals 9 hours, 32 minutes, and 44 seconds.

Science180: The Premier Organization that Scientifically Decoded the Origin of the Universe, Life, and Chemicals Accurately

When Baby Moon said goodbye to Baby Earth after Mother 3 birthed both, Baby Earth asked Baby Moon, *"Where are you going, my friend? I like you, don't leave me"*.

Baby Moon replied to Baby Earth, *"Don't worry, I will not be that far, I am just traveling for 9.53 hours to go to my own place. You can still see me anytime. Did you forget that when you were being born, I was pushed away, and that for both of us to exist, there is no way we can stay together"*?

Source: © 2025 by Nathanael-Israel Israel / www.science180.com

After saying goodbye to Baby Earth, Baby Moon traveled for 9.53 hours before crossing the 384,400 km and reaching the position of the Moon, where it took some additional time before being wrapped around into the Moon.

Figure 33: How long did Baby Moon travel after leaving Baby Earth before reaching the position of the Moon today?

When Baby Moon reached the position of the Moon, it was still looking like layers of water or spaghetti or noodles that needed to be wrapped around a fork so that Baby Moon could become the Adult Moon we know today. The length of the water layers of Baby Moon was as long as the perimeter or circumference of the Moon we know today. If you remember, I told you earlier that the distance from the center of a circle to the edge is called the "radius," and that using the radius, the perimeter, or circumference, can be calculated.

NASA has determined that the Moon's radius is 1738.1 kilometers. Using that number, my Daddy said the perimeter, or the distance around the Moon, is about 10,915.27 kilometers (see Figure 34).

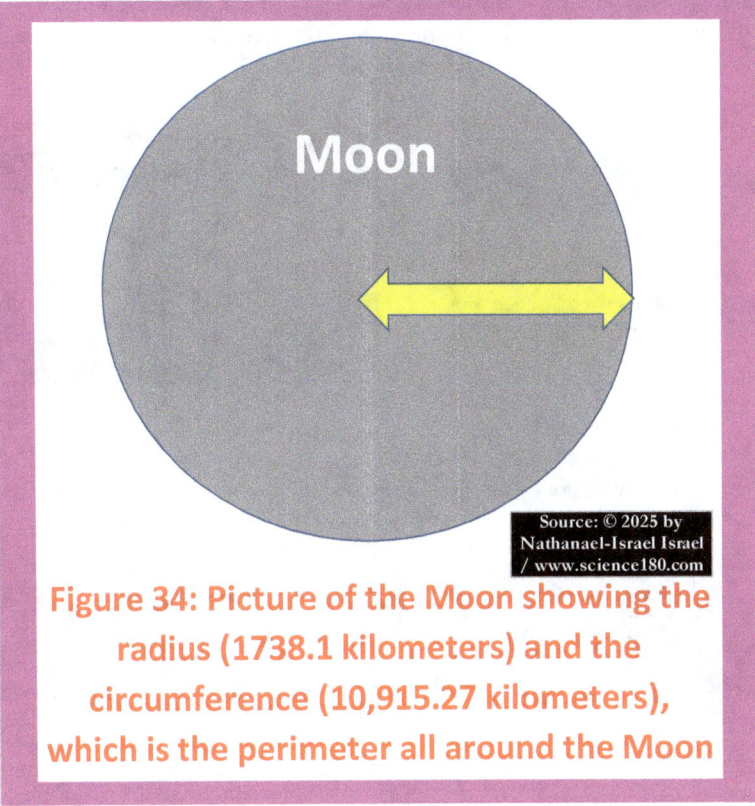

Figure 34: Picture of the Moon showing the radius (1738.1 kilometers) and the circumference (10,915.27 kilometers), which is the perimeter all around the Moon

Recalling the circumference (meaning the length of the perimeter of the Earth), Daddy said that the length of the water layers of the Baby Moon was about one-quarter that of the Earth. This means that the water layers of Baby Earth were about 4 times those of Baby Moon.

Now that we know the length of the water layers of Baby Moon that needed to be wrapped around like a fork, we still need to know the speed of that wrapping around. Again, based on some data collected by NASA, my Daddy has shown for the first time in history that the speed at which the water layers of Baby Moon were rolled around was about 1.022 kilometers per second (which is about 1 kilometer per second). That speed is called the orbital speed of the Moon.

As we did before, to know how long it took for the water layers of Baby Moon to be wrapped around, my Daddy divided the circumference of the Moon by the orbital speed of the Moon:

$$\frac{10,915.27 \text{ km}}{1.022 \text{ km/s}} = 2.97 \text{ hours}$$

In other words, as you can see in Figure 35, after Baby Moon arrived at the position of the Moon, it took around 2.97 hours for all its water layers to wrap around to form the Adult Moon we know today.

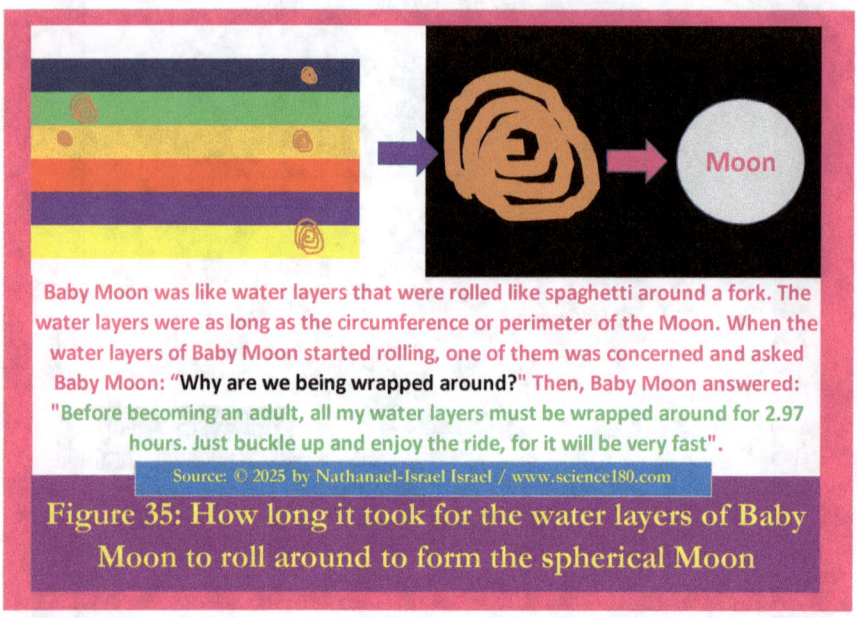

Baby Moon was like water layers that were rolled like spaghetti around a fork. The water layers were as long as the circumference or perimeter of the Moon. When the water layers of Baby Moon started rolling, one of them was concerned and asked Baby Moon: "**Why are we being wrapped around?**" Then, Baby Moon answered: "Before becoming an adult, all my water layers must be wrapped around for 2.97 hours. Just buckle up and enjoy the ride, for it will be very fast".

Source: © 2025 by Nathanael-Israel Israel / www.science180.com

Figure 35: How long it took for the water layers of Baby Moon to roll around to form the spherical Moon

A while ago, I told you that Baby Moon took about 9.53 hours to move from Baby Earth's position to the Moon's position. Then, once it reached the position of the Moon, it took about 2.97 hours for all its water layers to be wrapped around to form the Adult Moon we all know today. This means that the time it took for Baby Moon since it left Baby Earth, all the way to the time that Adult Moon was formed, was equal to:

$$9.53 \text{ hours} + 2.97 \text{ hours} = 12.5 \text{ hours}$$

In other words, after Mother 2 birthed Baby 3, which became Mother 3, meaning the Mother of the Earth and the Moon, it took about 12.5 hours before the Moon was fully formed as an adult.

I showed you earlier that after leaving Baby Sun, Mother 2 spent about 67.29 hours before giving birth to the Mother of the Earth and Moon. I just showed you that after Baby Moon was born, it took 12.5 hours for it to grow up and become the adult Moon we know today. To calculate the total amount of time that passed before the Moon was formed since the beginning, we need to add 67.29 hours to 12.5 hours. The result of this addition is about 79.8 hours. Because one day is 24 hours, 79.8 hours is equal to 3.32 days. Let's do some STEAM and lay out this sentence like a beautiful math formula:

Nathanael-Israel Israel: Author of "Reconciling Science and Creation Accurately"

$$\frac{79.8 \text{ hours}}{24 \text{ hours/day}} = 3.32 \text{ days}$$

In other words, the Moon was fully formed about 3.32 days after the beginning of the Solar System. By the way, 3.32 days means 3 days have passed, but 4 days have not yet passed. Therefore, 3.32 days means the 4th day. That is why scientific data show that the Moon formed on the 4th day after the beginning of the Solar System's formation. Figure 36 summarizes the process and the time it took for the Moon to be formed.

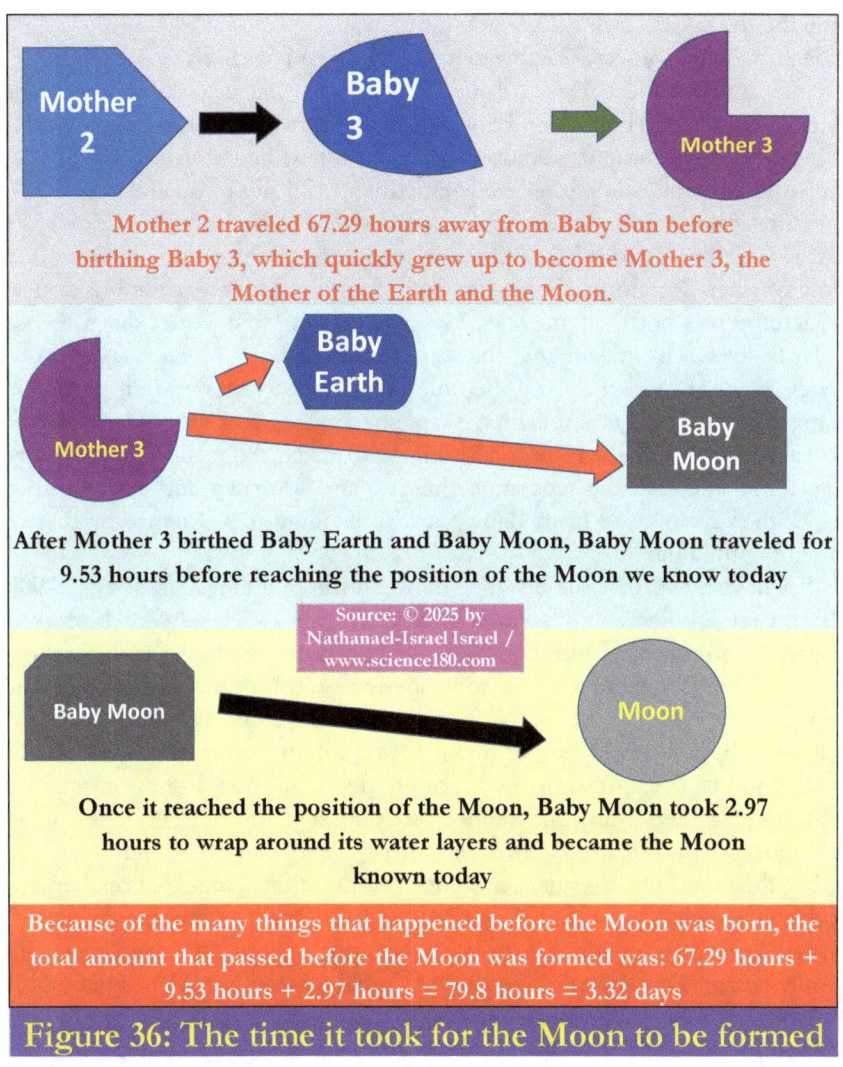

Figure 36: The time it took for the Moon to be formed

Science180: The Premier Organization that Scientifically Decoded the Origin of the Universe, Life, and Chemicals Accurately

21. How long did it take for the Sun to be formed?

I then asked Daddy, "How long did it take for the Sun to be born?"
Using the same math he did for the Earth and the Moon, Daddy helped me answer that question. As a reminder, we learned earlier that Mother Solar System gave birth to 2 babies:

- Baby 1 or Baby Sun, which grew up to become the Sun, and
- Baby 2, which grew up to become the Mother of all the celestial bodies orbiting the Sun.

The question we are trying to answer now is how long it took for Baby Sun to become the fully Adult Sun we know today.

Indeed, when Mother Solar System was pregnant with Baby 1 and Baby 2, it took some time for the babies to form. This means that it took some time before Baby Sun was born. Then, after Baby Sun was born, it also took some additional time (meaning more time in addition to the time that had already passed) for it to grow up and become Adult Sun. Are you getting me? I hope you are!

Let's first calculate the time it took for Baby Sun to be formed. Daddy has done a lot of research and proved that the time it took for Baby Sun to be born is about the time Mother 2 spent moving from Baby Sun and arrived at the position where Baby Mercury was born. By the way, Mercury was the first planet that was born in the Solar System. This means that the water layers of Baby Mercury were on top of the water layers of Mother 2. And the time Baby Mercury was born, it means that all the water layers of Mother 2 must have separated and moved away from Baby Sun.

To calculate the time it took for Mother 2 to reach the position of Mercury, we need to know the distance separating the Sun and Mercury, and also the speed at which Mother 2 ran away from Baby Sun. By dividing that distance by that speed, we can know the time.

NASA has shown that the distance between the Sun and Mercury is 57,909,000 km. If you are an elementary school student, I hope you tried your best and read this gigantic astronomical number as 57 million nine hundred and nine thousand kilometers. Even if you are not able to properly read this number, don't worry about it. We will do our best to be sure you understand the story. We know some people don't like math, but they like other things that mathematicians cannot do. We are all different, and just because someone is not good at math does not mean they are not good at anything else. Someone cannot be good at math, but very good at art, or other important things in life. In other words, some people are not very good at math, but they are still very smart, and they can do other things that mathematicians and other scientists cannot do. We need to learn how to humble ourselves and know that everybody on this Earth has something special they can share with the rest of the world! This special thing can be a great work of art, a great cultural thing, a great musical thing, a great technological thing, a great piece of handwork, and many more. Everybody is unique, and we don't need to keep comparing ourselves to others. Also, some people don't want to hear about math or science, yet they are enjoying our story. We enjoyed Daddy teaching us about science and life in general!

Daddy has demonstrated that Mother 2's speed of travel was about 617.6 kilometers per second. Before we continue, let me teach you some great scientific words. The 57,909,000 km separating the Sun and Mercury is called the semi-major axis of Mercury, which means the average distance separating Mercury and the Sun. The 617.6 km/s is what scientists have called the escape velocity of the Sun, which means the speed that things at the surface of the Sun must have before they can be able to escape or run away from the Sun without the gravity of the Sun pulling them back. In fact, just as the gravity of the Earth pulls things toward the Earth, so also the gravity of the Sun pulls things toward the Sun.

A long time ago, even before gravity formed, Baby Sun could also pull things toward its surface. This means that Baby Sun could have held Baby 2 close to it if Baby 2 was very slow, like a tortoise or a sloth. But, because Baby 2 was able to run away from Baby 1, Daddy had done some great math that showed that Baby 2 escaped or fled Baby Sun with the speed almost equal to the escape velocity of the Sun (617.6 kilometers per second). What I am saying here may sound silly or funny, but trust me, it took 10 years for my Daddy to dig deep into this crazy stuff until he got to the bottom of this difficult problem of the formation of the WHOLE universe. Did I tell you that my Daddy obtained his PhD or doctorate (a PhD is like grade 24) in science in the USA? For now, let's not worry about that, but get back to our math to know the time that has passed before Baby Mercury was formed.

Remember, we said that to calculate that time, we need to consider the distance separating the Sun and Mercury and also the speed with which Baby 2, which became Mother 2, fled Baby Sun. Here, the distance is 57,909,000 kilometers, and the speed is 617.6 kilometers per second. Therefore, the division that we need to do here is:

$$\frac{57,909,000 \text{ km}}{617.6 \text{ km/s}} = 26.05 \text{ hours}$$

In other words, my Daddy was the first person in the whole world to ever show that, since the beginning of creation, it took about 26.05 hours before Baby Sun was born. But this was not the Adult Sun we have today yet, for some changes happened to Baby Sun before it became the Adult Sun.

In fact, after Baby Sun was born, it looked like layers of fiery (meaning that they have fire) materials containing water or plasma organized like pancakes in a flowing river consisting of fire or burning stuff. Some of that stuff included water. In other words, although it is very hot, the Sun also contains water as of today. The layers of materials in Baby Sun needed to be gathered together before the Sun could be formed. Using the radius of the Sun, Daddy was able to calculate the length of the material layers of Baby Sun.

NASA has measured the Sun's radius and found it to be 695,700 kilometers. Doing some math, Daddy said that this radius implies that the circumference or perimeter or the distance all around the Sun is 4,368,996 kilometers (Figure 37). In other words, the layers of the materials in Baby Sun were about four million three hundred sixty-eight thousand, nine hundred, ninety-six kilometers long. Those layers of stuff were like spaghetti that needed to be wrapped around a fork.

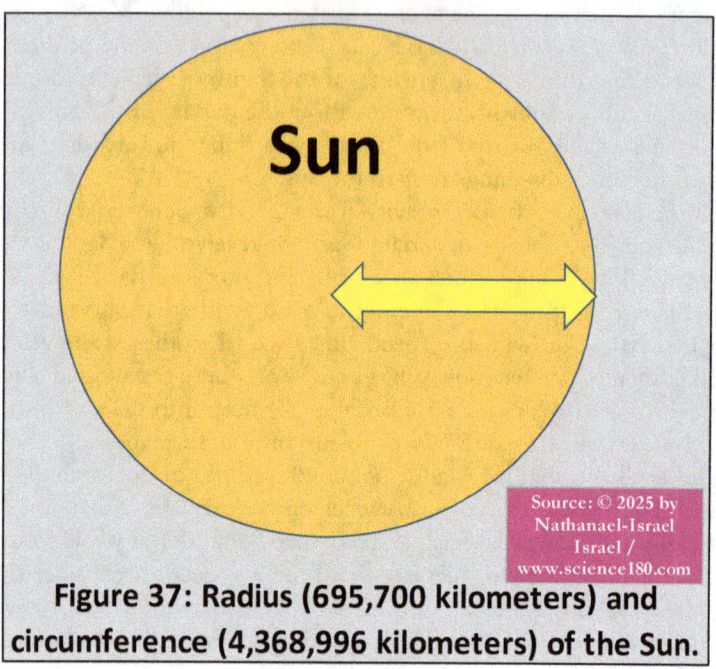

Source: © 2025 by Nathanael-Israel Israel / www.science180.com

Figure 37: Radius (695,700 kilometers) and circumference (4,368,996 kilometers) of the Sun.

To calculate how long it took for these layers to be wrapped around, we need to know the speed of that wrapping. Using some data collected by NASA, Daddy showed that the speed of the wrapping around was about 19.4 kilometers per second. That speed is also known as the Sun's speed relative to nearby stars. Like we did before for the Earth and the Moon, time is a distance divided by a speed. When Daddy divided 4,368,996 kilometers by 19.4 kilometers per second, he got 62.56 hours.

$$\frac{4,368,996 \text{ km}}{19.4 \text{ km/s}} = 62.56 \text{ hours}$$

In other words, after Baby Sun was born, it took about 62.56 hours for it to wrap around all its layers of material or plasma to become the Adult Sun as we know it today.

To calculate the total amount of time it took for the Sun to be fully formed, we need to add 26.05 hours (which was the time it took for Baby Sun to be formed) and 62.56 hours (which was the time it took for Baby Sun to mature or grow up to become the Adult Sun). The addition of these two times gives 88.6 hours:

$$26.05 \text{ hours} + 62.56 \text{ hours} = 88.6 \text{ hours}$$

This means that, from the beginning, it took 88.6 hours for the Sun to fully form. Because one day is equal to 24 hours, to know how many days are in 88.6 hours, Daddy divided 88.6 hours by 24, and the answer is 3.69 days:

$$\frac{88.6 \text{ hours}}{24 \text{ hours/day}} = 3.69 \text{ days}$$

By doing this math, Daddy showed that 3.69 days after the beginning of creation, the Sun was fully formed. The number 3.69 days means that 3 days had passed, but the 4th day was not finished yet. In other words, 3.69 days means that the Sun was formed on the 4th day. Those who finished or who are about to finish elementary school know that 3.69 days is a decimal that lies between 3 and 4, meaning a number that has a comma in it and which is greater than 3 but smaller than 4. All decimals have a whole and a fractional part. For 3.69 days, the whole is 3, and the fractional part is 0.69. In other words, 3.69 days = 3 days + 0.69 days. Hence, as you can see in Figure 38, the Sun was formed on the 4th day.

After Mother Solar System birthed its 2 children, it took about 26.05 hours before Baby 2 left Baby Sun (which was Baby 1). At that time, Baby Sun did not yet have a clear shape, but was a layer of plasma or other hot material that needed to be collected to form the Sun. Baby 2 would later grow up to become Mother 2, the Mother of all the bodies orbiting the Sun

After Baby 2 completely left Baby Sun, it took 62.56 hours for the plasma layers of Baby Sun to collect and form the spherical Sun.

Source: © 2025 by Nathanael-Israel Israel / www.science180.com

The total amount of time it took for the Sun to be formed was 26.05 hours + 62.56 hours = 88.6 hours, which is 3.69 days, meaning on the 4th day Since the beginning of the formation of the Solar System

Figure 38: How long it took for the Sun to be formed

I hope you like our STEAM explanation. Before we do anything else in this book, we will check whether the Earth, the Moon, and the Sun were really formed as the Bible says. This is a BIG deal!

Nathanael-Israel Israel: Author of "Reconciling Science and Creation Accurately"

22. Does the math we did in this book match the Biblical story of creation?

Before we say whether or not the story and math that we did in this book match the Biblical story of creation or not, we will first review what our math said. Then, we will compare it with what the Bible said about creation.

Based on the math we did using the scientific data that NASA has collected and that my Daddy, Dr. Nathanael-Israel Israel, has better analyzed, the Earth was fully formed on the 3rd day of creation, while the Moon and the Sun were fully formed on the 4th day (see Figure 39). During their formation, water layers were separated, moved over a long distance, and then gathered together to form round celestial bodies like planets, asteroids, the Sun, and other stars in the universe.

Figure 39: What the scientific data said about the birthdates of the Earth, the Moon, and the Sun.

Baby Earth → Earth

Scientific data show that the Earth formed on the 3rd day after the beginning. Most of this time was because Mother 2 had to travel a long distance before birthing Mother 3, the Mother of the Earth and the Moon

Baby Moon → Moon

Scientific data collected by NASA showed that the formation of the Sun and the Moon was finished on the 4th day since the beginning.

Most of the time that passed before the Moon was formed was because Mother 2 traveled a long distance before the Mother of the Earth and Moon was formed, and after baby Moon was born, it also took some time to move to its place before being collected into the Moon

Baby Sun

Source: © 2025 by Nathanael-Israel Israel / www.science180.com

Sun

It took almost 4 days for the Sun to form because the plasma layers of Baby Sun were huge and took a long time to wrap around.

This math was done for the first time in history by Dr. Nathanael-Israel Israel

In the end, the Earth was formed on the 3rd day, but the Moon and Sun were formed on the 4th day.

Now, let's look at what the Bible said about the creation of the Earth, the Moon, and the Sun.

In fact, the Bible said that the formation of the Earth was completed on the 3rd

Nathanael-Israel Israel: Author of "Reconciling Science and Creation Accurately"

day of creation. Before that, the Bible's Book of Genesis (chapter 1:6-13) said that there was a time when Baby Earth was filled with water and did not have a form. Then, the Bible said that the waters were collected together and, at one point, some covered the surface of the land. Then, God moved the waters on the surface so they could flow into the oceans, seas, rivers, ponds, lakes, creeks, and other waterways. All this happened on the 3rd day when the creation of the Earth was finished. In other words, the math we did using the data collected by NASA perfectly matched the Bible story of the creation of the Earth. In other words, the math we did using scientific data and the Biblical story of creation both indicated that the formation of the Earth was completed on the 3rd day. This means that the Biblical story of the formation of the Earth is true.

Now, let's see how the math we did for the Moon aligns with or contrasts with the Biblical account of the Moon's formation. My Daddy showed in a previous chapter that the Moon was formed 3.32 days after the beginning, meaning on the 4th day of creation. This is exactly what the Bible says in Genesis 1:14-19. In other words, the formation of the Moon, as shown using the scientific data, is exactly what the Bible said.

Last, let's compare the Biblical account of the Sun's creation with the scientific demonstration my Daddy did. As a reminder, I showed you in a previous chapter that the Sun was formed 3.69 days after the beginning of creation, meaning on the 4th day. This date is exactly when the Bible said the Sun was formed. One more time, the story, the Biblical story of the formation of the Sun, perfectly matches the scientific data. In other words, the creation story of the Sun is true. Figure 40 summarizes how the Biblical account of creation matches the scientific data.

Science180: The Premier Organization that Scientifically Decoded the Origin of the Universe, Life, and Chemicals Accurately

What the Bible said about the birthdate of the Earth, the Moon, and the Sun (Book of Genesis 1:14-19)

Baby Earth → Earth

The Bible said that the formation of the Earth was finished on the 3rd day of creation. Before that, the waters were divided from the waters, and some were collected to form the Earth.

The Bible said that the formation of the Sun and the Moon was completed on the 4th day of creation.

Baby Moon

Moon

Baby Sun

Sun

Source: © 2025 by Nathanael-Israel Israel / www.science180.com

Someone once asked the Moon and the Sun what their birthdate was. The Moon and the Sun answered: *"Don't you know the answer? In the first chapter of the Bible's Book of Genesis, Moses revealed, for more than 3500 years, that God created the Moon and the Sun on the 4th day of creation "*.

This math was done for the first time in history by Dr. Nathanael-Israel Israel

Figure 40: The Bible said in the Book of Genesis that the Earth was formed on the 3rd day, while the Moon and Sun were formed on the 4th day. This is exactly what Science confirmed based on the research of Dr. Nathanael-Israel Israel, a respected Beninese-American Scientist. Learn more at www.Israel120.com

To summarize, my Daddy, Dr. Nathanael-Israel Israel, showed for the first time in history that the date of the formation of the Earth, the Moon, and the Sun as recounted in the Bible is 100% correct and matches the date calculated using math and the data that top scientists, including those at NASA, have collected over the years. In fact, for many hundreds, and even thousands, of years, people from all

Nathanael-Israel Israel: Author of "Reconciling Science and Creation Accurately"

nations have been trying to understand how the universe was formed. Billions of dollars have been spent, but no real answer has been obtained until now.

All these facts prove that the Bible is correct and that the God of the Bible is really the Creator. By the way, the Biblical story of creation was written by Moses more than 3500 years ago. In those days, science did not exist, yet the details revealed by Moses were very accurate, meaning very precise. Daddy also told us that he has studied all other religions in the world, but none of them have a clear story of the creation of the universe whose details match the scientific evidence. In other words, of all the religious and scientific books in the world, only the Bible contains an original story of how the Universe was formed, just as the scientific data proved.

For the sake of history, Daddy said that before he closed this chapter, he needed to tell us something very important about some great scientists who lived before us and who have tried to understand the formation of the universe. Indeed, for more than 300 years, scientists have been trying very hard to get to the bottom of the problem of our origin. One of the greatest scientists of all time is Isaac Newton. He is from the UK, a country on the European continent. He was born in 1643 and died in 1727, meaning he died about 300 years ago. He tried to explain the origin of the universe, and he did a lot of work on gravity. But his efforts did not prove much things in the universe, but he was thinking the right way. Then, another scientist called Albert Einstein also tried to explain the universe, and he is most known for his work on relativity, something that is not the business of a little child, so you don't need to worry about. Although many people celebrate Einstein, Daddy said that he [Einstein] made a bigger mistake than Isaac Newton. Other great scientists were Galileo Galilei, Leonhard Euler, Nicolaus Copernicus, and Johannes Kepler, and each of these scientists told a story of the universe as they thought it had happened, and those stories are what scientists call theories. But none of them has demonstrated what my Daddy did. Otherwise, they could have explained how the Earth, the Moon, the Sun, and everything else in the universe were formed. In other words, until the research of my Daddy, Dr. Nathanael-Israel Israel, no human being has ever explained the formation of the universe properly. Some people even thought that the Bible was lying. Yet its story is true; it is people who failed to know how to explain it.

When Daddy came to this point, he turned to us and asked: *"How do you feel about the story and the fact that the Bible story of creation matches the scientific data?"* We all said that we feel very good and happy about the story. We also told Daddy that we are very proud of him. We thank God because we (Josephine Israel, Joelle-Major Israel, and Joshua-Enoch Israel) are the first children in the whole world to learn about this story and even to help our Daddy (Dr. Nathanael-Israel Israel) write a book about it! I hope you are enjoying the cool pictures we did.

The math and story in this book gave us greater confidence that the God of Israel is truly God. I am glad I know Him, and I have been believing in Him all my life. I will keep believing in Him forever and ever. Amen. Do you believe in God? If not, I encourage you to give your life to Him.

Science180: The Premier Organization that Scientifically Decoded the Origin of the Universe, Life, and Chemicals Accurately

What I shared with you in this book is just a small version or summary that children ages 7-12 could fully understand. My Daddy has written many other books on this topic, and if you want to know more, please consult his website at www.Science180.com or www.Israel120.com. Don't forget to subscribe to those subsites to learn more. By the way, we will still have a lot of great questions coming up. If you want to know the whole story, please keep reading. You don't want to miss what is coming up! Are you ready to learn more? If yes, let's go!

Before we talk more about the sections about God and Biblical creation, I would like to inform you that the other children's book that my dad wrote in 2025 (*"How Baby Universe Was Born"*) does not contain most of the information in the remaining portion of this book you are reading. So if you are reading this book, you don't have to read the other one I just mentioned. But those who read *"How Baby Universe Was Born"*) and those who want to know more about God in a language that children can understand must get this book you are reading now.

23. Is there any other cool scientific thing you can learn about the creation of the universe and God?

As you can see from my Daddy's demonstration, the scientific data points perfectly to God as the creator of the universe, just as the Bible says. Although Dad has a lot to say about God and the creation of the universe, he could not do so in the other children's book he wrote, for he didn't want to force people who don't believe in God to read it if they don't want to. At the same time, because we cannot reach this point of this book without bringing to people's attention the existence of this children's book that you are reading now, in which he addresses some deep questions children and adults usually ask concerning God and the Biblical creation. This book ("*How God Created Baby Universe*") will greatly benefit you. In it, Dad addressed other important questions, such as:

- Who and where is God?
- Who made God?
- What does He look like?
- What does heaven look like?
- When God spoke for things to appear during creation, where did they come from?
- When the animals were created, did they obey God's instructions?
- Where did God live before He created the heavens and the Earth?
- Where was God before creation?
- Why can't we live forever like God?
- How come everybody does not believe in God?
- How did God make heaven?
- How did God make Himself, and what material is He made from?
- How did God make the galaxies?
- Why did God take six days to create everything?
- Why does God live forever, but we, human beings, can't–or can we?
- How old is God?
- How old is the Earth?
- Before God created the first human beings, what was the universe like, and what was God himself like?
- Did God create any bad animals that can hurt people?
- Did God make doors, toys, and cars?
- Did God make hats so the Sun does not beat down on us?
- Did God make houses?
- Did God make the balls that we play with?
- Did God make TVs, and what shows does He watch?

Science180: The Premier Organization that Scientifically Decoded the Origin
of the Universe, Life, and Chemicals Accurately

- Do all animals obey God?
- How and why was darkness born?
- How are clouds made?
- How did plants sprout from the Earth for the first time, and why are they mostly green?
- How were human beings made, and where do babies come from?
- How did the first human beings look after they were formed?
- How were bones made, and why do birds fly but people cannot?
- How was the air we breathe made?
- How was the sky made, and why is it blue and black sometimes?
- How was time born, and why are the morning, the afternoon, and the evening different?
- How were angels formed?
- How were animals formed?
- How were seeds made?!
- Why are most plants green?
- How were the seas and the oceans made?

Won't it be cool if everybody could get the accurate answer to all of these questions?

Maybe you are wondering:

- Does the Bible scientifically teach anything else about the universe's origin that most people ignore?
- Is there any way for Christians to talk to evolutionists, Big Bang proponents, atheists, and all other freethinkers about the universe's formation so they will be very interested in knowing more about God?
- Is there a best way for believers to talk to stubborn rationalists about the universe's formation so they will beg to be led to God right away?
- Do you have to embrace evolution or deny God to scientifically prove that God created the universe in 6 literal days?
- Do Christians have to compromise with evolutionism to convince anyone about creation or the existence of God?
- Do you have to stop thinking to scientifically prove that God created the universe?
- Can anyone fix the trend according to which more people are denying God at the expense of secular theories because they think that it is impossible for science and faith to meet?
- Can anything be done to scientifically fix what is causing more and more college students to question the Bible, abandon their Christian faith, while kissing secular biology and physics books that program them to believe in evolutionism, the Big Bang, and other theories that deny God?

Nathanael-Israel Israel: Author of "Reconciling Science and Creation Accurately"

SECTION 3: POWERFUL MATH ABOUT HOW LONG IT TOOK TO FORM THE EARTH, THE MOON, AND THE SUN

- Is a church or a pastor making you doubt God or the Biblical story of creation?
- Is your school teaching about the origin of the universe, making you doubt creation?
- Is science making you doubt your faith?
- Is the Biblical account of creation making you doubt science?
- Is science making you doubt God or the Bible?
- Are science and the Bible really diametrically opposed or in conflict with each other?
- Is it true that the science versus the Bible debate will never be settled?
- Are science and the Bible really incompatible?
- Does the Bible really disagree with science?
- Is the Bible actually an obstacle to scientific progress?
- Is science being used to deny God?
- Can science affect our mind and faith?
- Why do secular rationalists and freethinkers think that Christians are irrational?
- What if Christians are not as irrational as secular rationalists and freethinkers think they are?
- What process can rationally explain the Biblical account of creation and remove all the roadblocks in the ways of previous scientists who tried to scientifically interpret the Genesis story?
- Is there any lie that most pastors spew from the pulpit about creation, and is there any simple scientific formula to accurately overcome it quickly without angering Christians, God, and the unbelievers?
- Can Biblical creation fuel your scientific success?
- Can creationists disagree with anti-creationists without angering anyone?
- Can atheists, rationalists, secularists, and freethinkers scientifically survive and heal from doubting God?
- What is the best way to think fully within the conflict between reason and faith?
- Which Biblical verses have the power to bring science to its knees–or can't they?
- Why do most people believe in and stick with incorrect universe-origin theories?
- Why does the discovery of the perfect link between science and Biblical creation of the universe mean good news for atheists, Evolutionists, and Big Bang proponents?

Besides the children's books in which you will find answers to some of those questions, my dad wrote other books for adults about the universe's creation that

Science180: The Premier Organization that Scientifically Decoded the Origin of the Universe, Life, and Chemicals Accurately

HOW GOD CREATED BABY UNIVERSE

can help you:
- *"Reconciling Science and Creation Accurately"*
- *"From Science to Bible's Conclusions"*

Later, I will talk about them and how people can get my dad to answer these questions and many more.

74
Nathanael-Israel Israel: Author of "Reconciling Science and Creation Accurately"

SECTION 4: IMPORTANT QUESTIONS ABOUT GOD

24. How did God make Himself and what material is He made from?

As we were learning about creation, we became very curious about knowing how God created Himself. We know that God created everything in the universe, and the scientific data also proves that. But how did He create Himself? My brother Joshua-Enoch asked Dad. Then, Daddy told him that it was a very good question, but very difficult to answer. In fact, my sister Joelle-Major and I wrote down the same question and were about to ask Dad.

Daddy told us that he does not know how God created Himself. He also said that he does not even think that God has a beginning. To put it the way the Bible said it, God is the Alpha and the Omega, meaning He is the beginning and the end. Daddy also told us that even if God has a beginning, it may be difficult to explain. Because we cannot see God with our own eyes, we don't know how tall He is. We also don't know whether He plays with toys like us or likes ice cream and cookies like us. We wondered if God eats cheeseburgers and if he plays in the mud or jumps on a BIG trampoline in heaven, and if that is what makes the thunder sound we hear during a storm. Daddy was laughing loudly when we asked those questions, for he felt like we were talking like children.

God is not a human being to be measured by His height, but if He wants to be tall, He can be taller than the WHOLE universe. God does not play with toys like children do, but He loves children and enjoys seeing them play and be happy. God does not eat food like us, for He cannot get hungry; therefore, He does not eat ice cream, cookies, or cheeseburgers. God does not play in the mud, and He is Holy, meaning He is very pure and no dirt or sin can touch Him. He does not jump on a trampoline in heaven, for he does not need to play to be happy or to satisfy Himself. He is perfect. Finally, God is not the one making the thunder sounds during a storm, but those are caused by clouds, heat, and winds in the sky.

Daddy told us that many very smart people have been trying to understand those questions and how the things we see around us were created, but they are still struggling to do so. It is much more difficult to explain how God, whom we do not see, created Himself. Because we cannot properly explain what we see, it is even more difficult to explain how God, whom we do not see, created Himself. That is why I do not try any harder to understand how God made Himself. What I know is that God made every person, animal, and plant, and I am thankful. I believe He is somewhere, He loves me, He sees me, and He can see everything at once and can do anything in one second. God is older than anybody and anything. From Adam and Eve until today, people have lived and died. God has been living before creating human beings and the universe, and He is still living and will never die.

Then, I asked Daddy: "*What material is God made from?*"

Daddy answered me that, although we never saw God, the Bible teaches us that God is fire. He is also a bright light, brighter than the Sun. His fire is hotter than lava. He can take any form and transform Himself into anything if He wants. For example, at one point, the Holy Spirit took the form of a dove to come down on Jesus when John the Baptist was baptizing him. God can also manifest Himself as a wind and as a lion. In fact, Jesus is called the Lion of the Tribe of Judah. God is Spirit; hence, we cannot see Him face-to-face with our eyes. For spirits are invisible. Just as you cannot see oxygen in the air, yet we breathe it, and it helps our bodies, so also we believe that God exists, although we cannot see him with our eyes. He is made of different materials than we and anything else on Earth.

Science180: Where Universe-Origin and Life-Origin Are Accurately Decoded, Full Stop

25. Where did God live before He created the heaven and the Earth?

This very important question was asked by me. Daddy started answering it by saying that every human being needs a home. Some people buy their own home. Those who cannot afford to buy a home rent a home or an apartment. God also has a home. But that home is not on this Earth or the Universe He created.

God's home is way beyond the universe. God was living there before creating the universe. Because God always lives, and we believe He has no beginning and no end, He always lives in His home, which we believe is a kind of heaven. To make it short, God's home is far above this universe. In fact, when God stays in His home, He puts His feet on the whole universe. The good news is that a day is coming when those who believe in God will live with Him in heaven forever and ever. AMEN!

"*How did God make heaven?*" Joshua-Enoch and Joelle-Major asked Daddy.

Daddy replied that he does not know all the details of how God made heaven, but he told us that God created everything. When people talk about heaven, they usually think about the place where God stays or the place where those who believe in God will stay forever in the presence of God. But the fact is that God created many heavens. The English translation of the Bible renders all instances of "heaven" with the same word. But in Hebrew (the language in which the Old Testament was written), different words are used to address each heaven. Daddy said that as we get older, he will write another book for us in which he will teach those details. For now, he said that he had already presented those details in the books he wrote for adults.

The Heaven that most people think God lives in was created by God as a nice place, where there is no problem, and everybody there is fine and happy. In heaven, nobody gets hungry, nobody gets sick, nobody is thirsty, nobody dies, nobody is tired, nobody steals, nobody cries like a baby, and nobody has any worry, for everything is taken care of in that place. In Heaven, nobody has school homework that needs to be done every evening. In Heaven, nobody has any bites or mosquito bites, which can itch. Nobody in Heaven does bad things. Heaven is very nice and beautiful, and its streets are in GOLD. I don't know where Heaven is, but I just believe it is there somewhere.

"*Is heaven already ready, or is God still making it?*" I asked. Daddy answered that Heaven is already created, but God is still building houses for us over there, just as big cities have new buildings being built all the time. As soon as a person begins to believe in God, God begins building a house for them in Heaven. Every time a believer does a good thing, God decorates their house more beautifully. In other words, the type of life you live on this Earth and the choices you make will determine the kind of house you will have in heaven if you make it there.

Those who don't believe in God don't have a house in heaven, and they will not go to heaven, but they will go to hell, which is a lake of fire.

Nathanael- Nathanael-Israel Israel: Acknowledged as the First Human Being that Scientifically Reconciled Science and Biblical Creation

SECTION 4: IMPORTANT QUESTIONS ABOUT GOD

FORM THE EARTH, THE MOON, AND THE SUN

"Will we go to Heaven when the house is ready?" Joshua-Enoch asked Daddy.

Daddy answered that we will go to heaven when God decides and when everybody who is supposed to go to heaven is ready. Many more people who will go to heaven are not born yet, and many more that will go to heaven are already dead, but they will be risen from the dead. Many who will go to heaven are already living on this Earth, and some don't even believe in God yet, but they will believe in Him someday. God is waiting for everybody to be ready and for all the houses in Heaven to be built before He comes back and takes us to Heaven, where the believers will be with Him forever and ever.

"Who is the last person to be born before we go to heaven?" I asked. Daddy answered that he does not know who that person will be, or when and where that person will be born. What matters for everybody is to believe in God and to be ready for that day.

Science180: Where Universe-Origin and Life-Origin Are Accurately Decoded, Full Stop

26. How was everything in the universe formed?

Now, Daddy will be answering three very important questions that we asked:

- How many creatures did God make?
- How did God say things, and how did they get created?
- How did God know the things He created were good?

God created millions of creatures. Human beings have tried to discover and name them. Yet, many are still unknown and may probably never be known. Some creatures live deep in the sea, in the oceans, and underground. Some are hidden in forests, bushes, and other places, even in jungles and deserts. Examples of creatures are plants, animals, bacteria, fungi (plants that look like mushrooms), and many others.

The main types of animals are mammals, reptiles, birds, fish, and insects. When we talk about animals, insects are the most abundant on Earth, meaning that there are more insects than any other kind of animal. Some creatures are angels that most human beings cannot see with their eyes. Yet, angels exist. In other words, many things are hidden from our eyes, and we just need to believe they are there.

A long time ago, before science was developed, people did not know things like bacteria and viruses. But as science grew and microscopes were invented, scientists were able to look deep inside living things to discover new details never known before. In the same way, the discovery of the telescope allowed scientists to look deep into the sky or space to find planets, stars, galaxies, and many other cool things. Therefore, in the future, many creatures, or things we ignore today, will be discovered. As scientists do some research, they discover new things, just like how using a magnifying glass can allow you to better see things that the naked eye cannot see. By the way, naked eyes do not mean eyes that have no clothes on, but just our natural eyes. Daddy felt like he needed to include this detail because when he talked about "naked eyes," Joshua-Enoch asked whether "dressed eyes" have clothes on, but "naked eyes" have no clothes. I hope you understand.

Let's answer the second crucial question that we asked Daddy: *"How did God know that the things He created were good?"*

In fact, the Bible said that God created the whole world using His word. This means that for everything God created, He just used His mouth to speak the word, and things were created. God is powerful and nothing is impossible for Him. When He speaks, everything listens and obeys, even rocks and other things that we think have no life. When He commands anything to become anything or to behave anyhow, it must happen. That is why the whole world was created according to God's will. Therefore, those who disobey God make Him "sad" and "mad" and will be punished one day if they don't repent. By the way, repent means knowing you have done wrong and deciding not to do it again, but also believing in God.

In our house, when I need anything, I ask Daddy, and he gives it to me. If we don't have it, we go to the store and we buy it. But because I did not know where the things that God created came from, I asked Dad: *"When God said things, where did they come from?"*

Nothing was formed anywhere before God told them to be, Daddy told me. In other words, the things God created were not in a store or storage room somewhere, then removed from that store to appear when God told them to. This means that before God created things, they were nowhere to be found. They were only present in God's thought. God spent some time planning everything before He started creating. Then, when God spoke the word, things just appeared. That is what creation means.

Although we are not God, there is power in the words that we speak. That is why we need to learn to confess good things to ourselves and to others and believe in ourselves. Otherwise, saying bad things to ourselves may make bad things happen to us because the words we speak have the ability to become some of the things we speak.

Before we started writing this book with Daddy, at one point, he asked us to read the Biblical story of creation in the first chapter of Bible's Book of Genesis and to come up with questions we have. He gave us this instruction after reviewing our first round of questions and noticing that we had a few questions about God. As we went back to read that story, we learned that God said that the things He created were good.

Therefore, my brother Joshua-Enoch asked Daddy: *"How did God know the things He created were good?"*

Daddy replied that because God is a good God, He cannot make anything bad. From the angels to human beings, passing through the plants, wild animals, planets, asteroids, satellites, and stars in the universe, everything God created was good. Even the Devil, who is bad today, was not created bad. He used to be called Lucifer and was a very good angel among all the other angels. He was a type of angel called a "Cherub." But one day, Lucifer disobeyed God, and started sinning and wanting to be like God. Therefore, God cast him out of Heaven.

Everything God created was for a reason. In the same manner, the light that God created on the first day was very good and is still very good. Light never disobeyed God, and it is still very good.

Science180: Where Universe-Origin and Life-Origin Are Accurately Decoded, Full Stop

27. Why did the Holy Spirit move over the surface of the water?

I read in the Book of Genesis that the Spirit of God moved upon the surface of the water on the first day of creation. I wondered why the Spirit of God was moving at the surface of the waters. What was the Spirit of God doing on the waters? I wondered. My curiosity led me to ask Daddy to help me understand.

Most people have read the Biblical story of creation, but they have not given it enough thought to properly understand it. Therefore, Daddy was excited that, at my age, I was trying very hard to comprehend deep things that the Bible said happened during the creation of the Earth.

Daddy told us that God moved upon the waters in a special way and direction, not only to form the Earth, but also to give it the power to produce living things. It is like how we mix soil with water to make mud balls that can be used to build things with our hands. The Holy Spirit touched the waters of Baby Earth to move and shape things just as a hand can move and shape things. During creation, God was not just sitting in Heaven, but He was moving over things he was forming and causing them to behave the way He wanted them to work. Hence, everything in nature is very organized. But sometimes, some people cannot understand the order in nature, and therefore, they think that many things are chaotic, yet they are very ordered.

Now that I understood why God was moving on the water, I did not understand how He gathered the water together. The Biblical story of creation also said that the waters were gathered together. Although Daddy was trying to explain to us how God collected the water of the baby celestial bodies, I did not fully understand. I tried many times to understand all the details of the creation story in the Bible, but I could not understand them all. For example, I did not understand how God gathered the water when it was liquid, and I cannot put it together myself like how I can put together houses and toys.

"Great point, Josephine," Daddy said, smiling at me for my intelligence and desire to learn about creation. Daddy continued by telling me that God has special skills and can do anything. If you remember the experiment that we did with the water bucket, we threw it into the air, and it was split into many water drops, which were moving. In the same way, in the beginning, Baby Universe had a lot of water, and, as it moved and was shaped, those waters were divided into many water bodies. Those water bodies were collected just as the water drops were separated when we threw water into the air. It is true that when people want to hold water in their hands, it leaks. But God's hand is different, and the way He separated and collected the water bodies together did not allow them to leak or go anywhere.

Daddy closed this question by making sure we understood that the question was very difficult and very important. He also told us that even people who went very far in school are still trying to understand it, but they are still struggling to explain it using science. Daddy told us that in the books he wrote for adults, he explained those questions better.

I then told Daddy that I am very proud of him for ensuring that we learn difficult things about creation from him in a language that all the children in the world can also comprehend. Joelle-Major and Joshua-Enoch also liked the story, and they, too, thanked Daddy. Hearing this, Daddy smiled, and we could see that he was very happy at our attitude. Daddy has always taught us to thank people who help us or do anything good to us.

Nathanael- Nathanael-Israel Israel: Acknowledged as the First Human
Being that Scientifically Reconciled Science and Biblical Creation

SECTION 5: HOW THE AIR, THE SKY, THE SEAS, THE OCEANS, AND CLOUDS WERE FORMED

SECTION 5: HOW THE AIR, THE SKY, THE SEAS, THE OCEANS, AND CLOUDS WERE FORMED

28. How was the air we breathe made?

This question was asked by my sister Joelle-Major. Before Daddy answered that question, he first explained to us why air is so important for human beings and most animals. In fact, the air we breathe is very important because without it, we cannot live. Our body needs air to function. Just like we need food to live, and without it we get hungry, we also need air so our bodies can function properly, meaning work properly. If people stop breathing, they will die. Therefore, every living human being must breathe, and those who cannot breathe by themselves have a breathing machine, which helps them to breathe. Or else they will die. After saying this, Daddy explained to us how the air was made.

The air we breathe is filled with many chemicals. Some of them are good for us, and others are bad. When God created the Earth, He ensured to put in it chemicals that we can breathe through our nose. God made those chemicals to be small enough so they could easily pass through our nose; otherwise, if they were too big or huge like balloons, they would have clogged or jammed our nose. In other words, if the chemicals in the air were big like balloons, they could not enter the nose, but after people manage to suck them toward the nose, there could be a traffic jam of chemicals by our nose. It is like a very big airplane trying to enter a house. It cannot enter. A bike can pass through the door of a house, but not an airplane or a boat.

Daddy has spent years studying how chemicals are made. He discovered that all chemicals were once babies that grew up and changed their shape to become the adult chemicals we know today. He told me that explaining the formation of chemicals and all the chemistry going on in the air to children my age is very difficult, but that as I grow up and learn more at school, he will tell me more. In the past, I used to think that there was nothing in the air, but now, I know there are many things that I cannot see in the air with my eyes. Before Daddy closed this question, he told us that today, plants play a huge role in helping nature clean the air. Plants produce oxygen, one of the main chemicals in the air. Examples of other chemicals in the air are nitrogen and hydrogen.

When human beings breathe, they take in oxygen and reject another type of gas called carbon dioxide, which is made of chemicals called carbon and oxygen. Carbon dioxide is toxic to human beings but not to plants. When plants absorb carbon dioxide, they produce oxygen and use the carbon to make the vegetables and fruits that we like. Plants also absorb or take water and other nutrients from the soil. Just as human beings need food to eat and water to drink, plants also need water and nutrients from the soil and the air.

As Daddy was answering Joelle-Major's question about how the air we breathe was formed, I wondered and asked Daddy if God had also given bugs noses to breathe in and out. Daddy replied that every living thing that God created has special needs, such as food, water, and air. If living things do not have those needs met, they will starve and die. Most animals breathe air through their nose. Even bugs have a nose. But their nose is very small. Some animals breathe through their skin. Even human

Nathanael- Nathanael-Israel Israel: Acknowledged as the First Human Being that Scientifically Reconciled Science and Biblical Creation

SECTION 5: HOW THE AIR, THE SKY, THE SEAS, THE OCEANS, AND CLOUDS WERE FORMED

beings take in and out of air through their skin, but this is not as effective as breathing through the nose.

29. How was the sky made, and why is it blue and black sometimes?

The sky is the blue we see above Earth's surface when we look high into space. At night, when we look up at the sky, we can see stars, the Moon, and some planets, such as Mercury, Venus, Mars, Jupiter, and Saturn. We tried to figure out where the sky came from and why it is so big, but we could not find the answer by ourselves. We then asked Daddy many questions about the sky:

- How was the sky formed?
- Why is it so big and blue?
- Why does the sky switch color when it gets dark?

Because the questions we asked were very important, Daddy was very proud of us for wanting to know more about the sky. To answer these questions, Daddy reminded us of what he taught us about the formation of the Solar System. Indeed, we learned that Mother Solar System birthed 2 children:

- Baby 1, also called Baby Sun, which grew up to become the Sun, and
- Baby 2, which grew up to become Mother 2, the mother of all the celestial bodies orbiting the Sun.

"Do you remember that?" Daddy asked us. We answered *"yes"*.

Smiling at us, Daddy continued the review by saying that Mother 2 traveled for a certain distance before birthing its children. Between two babies, Mother 2 traveled for a certain distance before being ready to give birth its children. In other words, the babies of Mother 2 were not born in the same place, but Mother 2 traveled for a certain distance before birthing each baby.

The blue sky we see when we look up, particularly when there is no cloud, is because of the huge distance separating the babies of Mother 2 and the babies of the other stars in the Universe. In other words, the sky we see around the Earth is not just formed from the babies of Mother 2, but also from the babies of the stars we see with our eyes. In fact, the universe is much bigger than the sky we see at night. The sky we see at night is to space what a drop of water is to the oceans.

The distance between the Earth and the Moon is due to the distance traveled by Baby Moon after it left Baby Earth. Remember that, at one point, the Earth and the Moon were once babies of Mother 3, the Mother of the Earth and the Moon. After the Mother of the Earth and the Moon grew up, they gave birth to Baby Earth and Baby Moon. Then, Baby Moon traveled for a certain distance before reaching a point when it became the Moon. Hence, the huge distance between the Moon and the Earth is due to the long journey that Baby Moon traveled after splitting from Baby Earth.

If you can remember the experiment that we did when we threw water into the air, it broke into water drops separated by some distance. In the case of the babies of the celestial bodies, the distance between them can be seen in the sky. In other words, if the planets, asteroids, and the star (the Sun) in the Solar System can be considered like big water drops, the huge space between them is like the distance between their baby water drops.

When we look at the sky, the stars are located very far from us because Baby Universe was very huge, and when baby galaxies and baby stars were popping up everywhere like popcorn, a huge distance separated them. For those babies moved at a very high speed, more than the speed of a racecar or the speed of a cheetah. When we look at stars in the sky, we may think that they are not moving, but in fact, they are moving very fast, and it is the huge distance separating them from us that makes us think that they are not moving. In the same way, when we see stars, planets, and asteroids in pictures, they seem very close. This is because the pages of the books that contain these pictures are small, and everything is scaled or made to fit those pages. That is why the vast distances between celestial bodies cannot be fully represented in pictures. Even the pages of those pictures will be as vast as the sky itself.

"Atmosphere" is a big word used to mention the air and gases that surround the Earth. The sky is sometimes black when fewer stars are visible due to atmospheric clouds. When fewer clouds are in the sky, the stars shine their light on the Earth. When the sky is cloudy, the clouds block the light of the sky, and it cannot reach the Earth. Hence, the sky is dark on cloudy nights.

Some stars are bigger than the Sun, yet their light is dim, or blurry, or unclear, or faint because these stars are very far from us. For when things are very far from us, they appear very small, or cannot be seen at all.

The white light is made of many colors, such as blue, violet, yellow, red, etc. The white light can be scattered and give the different lights it contains, such as the colors in a rainbow. During the day, sunlight shines on chemicals and particles in the sky. As it hits particles in the sky, the light does not continue in its original direction; instead, the particles scatter it, meaning they separate it and throw it in many directions depending on the type of light. Some particles or chemicals in the sky scatter or throw in many directions the blue light more than other kinds of light. Because blue light is scattered in the sky by particles, the sky is sometimes blue.

During the day, the Sun shines its light on the Earth, and we see daylight, but at night, the Sun is on the opposite side of the Earth. Because we cannot see the Sun at night, the sky is dark. Some people think that, in the night, the Sun is sleeping, but now I learned from Daddy that the Sun never sleeps.

Hearing this, Joelle-Major asked Daddy: "Where does the Sun go when it goes down at night?"

I jumped into the boat to come to her rescue by telling her that the Sun does not go anywhere because it stays almost at the same spot, but it is just the Earth that is moving around the Sun. Then, because she was not sure of my answer, she turned to Daddy and asked him if I was correct. "Yes, of course, Josephine was correct," Daddy replied. In fact, although the Sun slightly moves around itself, a movement called "wobbling," meaning it moves left and right and left and right as it turns all around the center of the Solar System.

Daddy added that the entire Solar System is moving through space, but we cannot just feel it. In other words, the Sun and everything orbiting it are moving through space. No celestial body is standing still in space. Everything is moving.

In summary, the sky was formed as the Mothers of the celestial bodies gave birth to their babies, which were separated by different distances.

Nathanael- Nathanael-Israel Israel: Acknowledged as the First Human Being that Scientifically Reconciled Science and Biblical Creation

30. How were the seas and the oceans made?

The seas and oceans are the largest bodies of water on Earth. Examples of seas are the Red Sea (which is located off the coast of Egypt) and the Mediterranean Sea (which is located between Northern Africa and Southern Europe). The Atlantic Ocean separates America and Africa. Every time Daddy takes my family to the beach, we are amazed at how huge the Atlantic Ocean is. The Indian Ocean is located South of Asia and east of Africa. The Pacific Ocean lies west of North America. By the way, the deepest part of the ocean is called the Challenger Deep and is in the Pacific Ocean, at the Mariana Trench, about 200 miles (322 kilometers) southwest of the US territory of Guam. There, the ocean is about 36,000 feet (meaning 10,973 meters) deep. The Mariana Trench is about 1580 miles (meaning 2542 kilometers) long and about 43 miles (or 69 kilometers) wide. That is very huge.

"*How were the seas and the oceans made?*" Joelle-Major asked. Daddy replied that, in the beginning, when the Earth was forming, it was covered by water at one point. Baby Earth had to be cracked open so the water that was covering it could go inside the big crack or big ditch. The crack was like a huge mouth at the Earth's surface, opened to swallow water. As more water entered the big crack or hole, it separated the continents and the dry lands, and the water of Baby Earth was collected into the oceans and seas. Some water also went into the rivers and lakes. By the time the Earth was fully formed, the surface of the land covered by the oceans and seas was more than two-thirds of the surface of the Earth. This means that the surface of the Earth is mostly water.

To wrap it up, oceans and seas were formed when the waters that were covering Baby Earth went inside the crack of Baby Earth so that the dry land could appear and Baby Earth became Adult Earth.

Nathanael-Israel Israel: Author of "How God Created Baby Universe"

31. How are clouds made?

This question came from Joelle-Major. Clouds are like white, gray, and black things in the sky that usually give rain. They start like gases that rise into the atmosphere and come together to form water, which then falls down like rain. Sometimes, the water in the clouds can become solid and fall down as hail.

Clouds are formed when a lot of water evaporates, meaning it rises from the surface of the earth or oceans or seas to go up into the sky. There, the clouds meet some conditions that allow them to become liquid water. These conditions can be the right temperature, the right amount of cloud, the right amount of pressure, the right amount of wind, the right amount of humidity, etc.

Clouds have many shapes. Some look like lions, others appear like angels, and others like bunnies, and many other shapes. Sometimes, when the right conditions are not met in the sky, clouds cannot become rain. That is why the sky is sometimes cloudy, yet no rain falls. But when the right conditions are met, the clouds can give rain and sometimes cause big storms like hurricanes and tornadoes.

Sometimes, when the sky is cloudy, thunder and lightning can pop up, and they can be fun to watch, but they can also be scary. Sometimes, it is very dangerous to be outside during a lightning storm, as lightning bolts can strike and injure people. That is why, although we would enjoy playing outside in the mud when it is raining, Daddy does not want us to do so all the time. He let us play in the rain only once, and he was right by us, watching and playing with us in our backyard. It is better to be safe than to try to have fun in the rain and find ourselves struck by lighting and end up in the hospital.

SECTION 6: HOW DARKNESS AND TIME WERE BORN

32. How and why was darkness born?

Darkness dominates most nights and it makes the night dark. When it is dark, we cannot see, but when light shines in the darkness, darkness disappears or stops existing. A very important question, whose answer we were unable to find was where darkness comes from. Therefore, Joelle-Major asked Daddy: *"How did God make darkness?"*

Replying, Daddy said that, in the beginning, darkness was everywhere in the universe. God created the darkness before the light so it could dominate or be the boss wherever light is absent. Usually, when it is dark, it is colder or warmer than when it is day. It means that the darkness of the night also helps cool down the Earth when it is, for instance hot in the summer. The darkness of the night also helps plants to grow and people to sleep. Imagine the night being clear like the day. It will be hard to sleep well. It will be hard for me to sleep at night when the light is on in my room. In the same manner, if the night sky was not dark, it would have been hard for some people to sleep. That is why most people usually turn the light off before they go to bed. In other words, darkness is not a bad thing.

Another thing that Daddy taught us about darkness is that it helps to cool down the night. During the day, the Sun shines on the Earth and makes us hot. But in the night, when the Sun is on the opposite side of us, the darkness of the night helps reduce the temperature. Without the darkness of the night, the temperature of the night could be very high and it may be difficult to live on Earth. God made the darkness to help us. He also made the light to help us see. It is hard to see when it is dark, but easy to see when there is light.

Although we cannot see in the darkness, it is a good thing because we are not supposed to see all the time. It is important to give our eyes some break or rest. Just like we cannot work all the time, it is also good for our eyes not to see all the time. If people's eyes can still be open and see when they are sleeping, they could dream crazy things and scare people. Their eyes can become very tired and sick because they are not resting. What I am saying is that darkness is not all bad. It is true that in the darkness, bad things can happen and some bad creatures can hurt, but let's keep in mind that darkness is also useful for a reason.

When I was reading the Bible, I learned that in the story of Genesis, God separated the darkness from the light. But because I did not understand that part of the story, I asked Daddy to explain to me how God separated the day from the night when He was creating the world. When replying, Daddy told us that, because the Earth rotates, when one of its sides is in the light, meaning facing the Sun, the other side is in the night. The rotation of the Earth allows the night to be somewhere different than the light. For example, when people in the US are in the day, people in China are in the night, and vice versa. This is because the US and China are on opposite sides of the Earth.

In our house, the light switch helps us to chase away the darkness. That is why when we turn the light on, the darkness disappears. But when we turn the light off, the darkness appears again. The same thing happens when the Sun rises and when it goes down. One way that God could have separated the light from the darkness is to cause the Earth to rotate so that the light and the darkness can stay on opposite sides. Another way to see this is to consider the power God gave the light to always dominate the darkness in such a way that the darkness always runs away wherever a light shines.

Science180: Understand the Origin of The Universe and Life. Increase Your Glory and Peace of Mind

33. How was time born, and why are the morning, the afternoon, and the evening different?

I have noticed that most things in nature are changing. For example, in the morning, the Sun rises; at noon, it is overhead; and in the evening, it goes down. But as we learned earlier, the Sun does not sleep, and it is not really correct to say that it rises or goes down.

I don't like the Sun to beat me too much, particularly at noon, for it hurts. But I like the nice evening weather. I don't like the crazy cold of winter either, nor the crazy heat of summer that can burn like a coal. However, I enjoy the spring when flowers are showing their glory. I also like the fall, particularly when leaves are falling, for they look like a celebration.

"Why did God make the time like morning, afternoon, and evening to be different?" I asked Daddy. I then learned that, because the position of the Sun above the Earth changes throughout the day, the temperature of the Earth also changes. The amount of light the Earth receives from the Sun also varies or changes throughout the day. That is why it is very hot at noon, but usually nicer in most mornings and evenings than in most middays. In other words, the changes we feel throughout the day as the Earth rotates or throughout the seasons of the year as the Earth orbits the Sun cause us to feel that the time is changing. If nothing was changing around us, it may be difficult for us to know that the time is passing. The passing of time gives us days, weeks, months, and years. It also helps us know our birthdate so we can celebrate!

The weather changes from one season to another because, as the Earth moves around the Sun, the conditions on Earth change. Hence, all the days are not the same. Just as the morning is different than noon, which is different from the evening, so also the fall is different from the winter, which is different from the spring, which is different from the summer. Each season has its mission, and together, they help us enjoy life on Earth.

As Daddy was explaining the changes of time and seasons to us, Joshua-Enoch raised his hands. I knew he had something important to ask. *"How did God make clocks that people use to know the time?"* he asked Dad. Daddy responded that God did not make clocks; human beings did. Human beings use the Sun and the Moon to define time. By looking at the position of the Sun and the Moon in the sky, people can guess what time it is.

SECTION 7: PLANTS, SEEDS, AND FOOD FORMATION

34. How did plants sprout from the Earth for the first time, and why are they green?

Joelle-Major was the one who asked this wonderful and great question. Daddy responded that there are many plants on Earth. Some are tall, others are short. Some, like watermelon, can be eaten like food, while others, like poison ivy, cannot be eaten. Whether they can be eaten or not, all plants were created from soil and water.

Being very powerful, God commanded the soil to bear plants, and it obeyed. Therefore, at the beginning of plant formation, Baby plants of various kinds sprout, just as seeds can germinate and give rise to plants that grow into adults and produce fruit. In other words, for plants to form, something began germinating in the soil, like a seed, and then that thing grew and developed into the different parts of a plant. This means that each plant we see today started like a baby when its great-great-grandparent was formed. Each Baby plant was not an adult yet, but it grew into a fully grown plant. In other words, all the Baby plants at the beginning grew up to become the adult plants we see today. Some Adult plants produced seeds, which will later germinate to give more plants. Some plants don't flower, yet they have their ways of giving birth to their babies.

Most plants we see today are not the same as those God formed in the beginning, but they are the descendants of those original plants. Most plants die after a growing season, which is less than a year. Even plants that are called perennials, meaning capable of living for many years without dying, most of those formed in the beginning may have died by now, and it is only their children that are alive today. Many plants have also disappeared, meaning they exist no more, because human beings have not taken good care of them, or because the environment was not good for them. In other words, we have fewer plants in the world today than we had in the beginning when all plants were created and living a happy life.

My Daddy, Dr. Nathanael-Israel Israel, has written books that scientifically explain in detail how plants were made. But for children like my sister, my brother, and me, he said that he would not go into certain details that only adults can understand. That is why Daddy decided not to go into some details here, and we were content with the summary he gave us.

Then, with a mind that likes to think a lot, Joelle-Major asked Daddy: "*Why are plants green?*"
Daddy replied that, although most plants are green, some plants are red, others are yellow, and some are purple. Some plants stay green all year long, and some of them are called evergreens.

Most plants stay green because of a chemical in them called chlorophyll. Chlorophyll allows plants to absorb sunlight. As I said earlier, there are many colors in the white light. Most plants don't absorb the green part of light, but they diffuse or reflect it, meaning they reject it. Because the green light is not absorbed by the plants, it colors them green. In other words, it is not that chlorophyll is green, but it does not absorb or take in the green part of the light that shines on plants. Therefore, the green portion of light is reflected or not taken in by plants; hence, it is seen on the leaves, which have the chlorophyll.

Green plants can lose their chlorophyll. As plants lose chlorophyll, their green color decreases. That is why in the fall, most plants change color. Leaves of some trees turn from green to yellow, orange, and red in the fall. And we like it because it is really pretty. When most of the chlorophyll is gone, the plants lose their green color and usually die and fall. Flowers have different colors because of the chemical composition of their tissues. My favorite flowers are sunflowers and marigolds, while my sister Joelle-Major's favorite flowers are daisies and marigolds. My brother Joshua-Enoch's favorite flowers are roses and zinnias.

Science180: The Best Way to Properly Explain the Universe Creation & Life Creation Using Science

35. How were seeds made?

I just told you that some plants can produce seeds, but others cannot. But I did not tell you yet how seeds were made. Thanks to a question my brother Joshua-Enoch asked Daddy about that matter, I will now tell you how the first seeds were ever made.

When I eat watermelon, apples, cucumbers, avocados, lemons, corn, grapes, strawberries, pomegranates, and other fruits we have in our garden, I find seeds in them. Those seeds are different. Some are small; others are big. Some are soft, but others are hard. For instance, I can eat cucumber seeds and corn seeds without problems, but avocado seeds are too hard to break with my teeth.

Because I have already lost some teeth, and I have gaps between my teeth, I don't want to break my other teeth by eating seeds that are very hard. I remember a day when I lost my tooth; people said I was cute, and my smile made them smile. But it was hard to eat my apple without my front teeth. Daddy, who likes to chew on bones with his teeth to get the flavor out later, told me that when people get old and lose teeth, their teeth don't come back, but they have to stay like that unless they get fake teeth like some grandpas who can make some funny faces using their fake teeth. Some people can also take them out of their mouths whenever they want.

All seeds were created by God because He wanted plants to continue growing. For example, my Daddy has a garden in our yard, and every year, he plants seeds so we can harvest them later. If we don't plant a seed of a plant, we won't harvest that plant. For example, if we plant corn, we will harvest corn. If we don't plant tomatoes, we cannot harvest tomatoes later. An apple seed cannot produce an onion.

My Daddy told me that God created seeds from the soil in a way my brain cannot fully understand yet. God created seeds for each plant so that people and animals can enjoy and eat them. We enjoyed helping our parents work in our garden, and we learned many tricks and skills. We planted many flowers in our yard and enjoy seeing them grow. Many insects (such as bees and butterflies) also come to eat the flowers' nectar (something sweet in flowers). We enjoyed looking at the beautiful flowers as the insects got their food. During those times in the garden, Daddy told us a lot of funny stories. Very soon, I will tell you one of those stories about cucumbers and tomatoes. Because this is our favorite story, we insisted that Daddy put it in this book. Because we thought it was a silly yet funny story, we even asked Daddy to put it at the beginning of the book, but he said it was better to place it where we discuss plants. I hope you enjoy it!

SECTION 8: CAN YOU BELIEVE THAT DADDY'S TOMATOES AND CUCUMBER TRAVELED TO HEAVEN?

36. How did God make food?

When Daddy asked us to write down our questions about how the universe was formed, I came up with 50, Joelle-Major had 30, and Joshua-Enoch had 20. One of Joelle-Major's questions was how God made plants.

Daddy answered her by telling us that when God was creating everything, He knew a day would come when people would get hungry. So, He decided to create certain plants that can give food. In the beginning, God spoke the word, and all the plants that produce food were created. But after creation, God did not create food as He did in the beginning. Today, plants grow from seeds, and when they reach a certain stage, they produce crops, vegetables that can be eaten. Before they produce fruits, plants, and flowers. Then some flowers grow into becoming fruits.

Farmers grow most of the plants people eat. Some crops are eaten raw, while others are cooked, and other things are mixed with them before they can be eaten. Even so, how a plant grows from a seed to fruits that can be eaten is a big miracle. Some people grow their food themselves, but most people have to go to the store to buy it, then wash it and eat. Some foods are also washed and packaged, ready to be eaten.

Joshua-Enoch's favorite fruits are bananas, avocados, corn, apples, and watermelons. My favorite fruits are grapes, pomegranates, oranges, peaches, apples, and cantaloupe. Joelle-Major's favorite fruits are apples, oranges, plums, watermelons, corn, and tomatoes. Everybody in my family loves lettuce.

My dad grows all of those fruits in our garden. My sister and I love watching our dad work in the garden to produce all of these plants. We used to just watch Daddy, but as we are growing, we started helping Daddy a little. Sometimes, we bring him water so he can drink and cool down when it is too hot outside. Daddy likes to work very hard in our garden, and we like to share some of our vegetables and fruits with our neighbors, friends, and the homeless.

When Daddy is working in the garden, he usually lets us jump on the trampoline and play games. But when it is too hot, he lets us stay under the tent so the Sun does not beat us. Sometimes, he plants things in the rain, and when it rains, we always stay inside as he works. When he worked outside, and we were not near him, he always opened the blind of our window and rolled the window down so we could talk to him if we needed anything. He usually tells us that one day, we will have to start helping him more in the garden. Therefore, as I grow up, I plan to help Daddy more in the garden so that I can learn how to grow most plants. This is because I plan to have my own garden one day. But for now, even when we ask him to help in the garden, he does not want us to mess with it yet, for we are still learning as we watch. We know the names of more than 20 vegetables and fruits that Daddy planted in our garden. He has planted apple, pear, peach, plum, orange, tangelo, grapefruit, pecan, avocado, lemonade, muscadine grape, olive trees, etc. Now, I will tell you a very important and interesting story of the cucumber and tomato that Daddy has in our garden.

101

Science180: The Best Way to Properly Explain the Universe Creation & Life Creation Using Science

Nathanael-Israel Israel: Known as the Outside-Of-The-Box Universe-Origin
Scientist

SECTION 8: CAN YOU BELIEVE THAT DADDY'S TOMATOES AND CUCUMBER TRAVELED TO HEAVEN?

SECTION 8: CAN YOU BELIEVE THAT DADDY'S TOMATOES AND CUCUMBER TRAVELED TO HEAVEN?

Science180: The Place Where the Accurate Interpretation of Universe-Creation and Life-Creation Data Matters

37. Do you want to hear about why a tomato and a cucumber begged a human being not to eat them?

You are about to read a very nice, creative story. All the children who listened to this very important story loved it and wanted to hear more. Some children even called it the coolest Baby Universe story ever.

- Do you want to listen to that story?
- Have you ever heard of plants talking to a human being?
- Did you ever think about plants organizing a meeting so they can send one of them to meet God?
- How can plants travel?
- Even if plants can travel, do you think they can travel as far as heaven?
- Will they take a train, an airplane, a boat, a car, or a bike?
- Or will they just walk or run as they go on that long journey?

If you want to learn about the coolest story ever, let's go!

The story goes like this. One day, when COVID-19 hit the world, Daddy decided that to have fresh vegetables and eat comfortably at home, we needed to grow our own garden. Therefore, we went to the store to buy seeds for tomatoes, cucumbers, squash, zucchini, Swiss chard, lettuce, green peppers, cayenne peppers, jalapeños, watermelon, corn, parsley, cantaloupes, sage, basil, carrots, etc.

Figure 41: Carrot from Daddy's Garden. © 2025 by Nathanael-Israel Israel / www.Israel120.com

Figure 42: Corn. © 2025 by Nathanael-Israel Israel / www.Israel120.com

Figure 43: Green pepper. © 2025 by Nathanael-Israel Israel / www.Israel120.com

Figure 44: Tomato sleeping under its leaves. © 2025 by Nathanael-Israel Israel / www.Israel120.com

Figure 45: Some vegetables we harvested in Daddy's Garden. © 2025 by Nathanael-Israel Israel / www.Israel120.com

Figure 46: Tomato from Daddy's Garden. © 2025 by Nathanael-Israel Israel / www.Israel120.com

Figure 47: Some vegetables from Daddy's Garden. © 2025 by Nathanael-Israel Israel / www.Israel120.com

Figure 48: Tomato from Daddy's Garden. © 2025 by Nathanael-Israel Israel / www.Israel120.com

Figure 49: Basil from Daddy's Garden. © 2025 by Nathanael-Israel Israel / www.Israel120.com

Figure 50: Lettuce from Daddy's Garden. © 2025 by Nathanael-Israel Israel / www.Israel120.com

Figure 51: Broccoli. © 2025 by Nathanael-Israel Israel / www.Israel120.com

Science180: The Place Where the Accurate Interpretation of Universe-Creation and Life-Creation Data Matters

Figure 52: Turnip. © 2025 by Nathanael-Israel Israel / www.Israel120.com

Figure 53: Swiss chard. © 2025 by Nathanael-Israel Israel / www.Israel120.com

SECTION 8: CAN YOU BELIEVE THAT DADDY'S TOMATOES AND CUCUMBER TRAVELED TO HEAVEN?

Figure 54: Red cabbage. © 2025 by Nathanael-Israel Israel / www.Israel120.com

Figure 55: Cabbage. © 2025 by Nathanael-Israel Israel / www.Israel120.com

Science180: The Place Where the Accurate Interpretation of Universe-Creation and Life-Creation Data Matters

Figure 56: Watermelon. © 2025 by Nathanael-Israel Israel / www.Israel120.com

Daddy started a nursery, and after the seeds germinated, he transplanted them, meaning he put them into another place where they have more room and can grow better. Then, Daddy watered them every day. After a few days, Daddy also gave them plant food. He also ensured they had enough Sun.

Soon, the plants started growing higher and higher. As the plants were growing, they were happy. They showed their joy through their beautiful leaves and flowers. The happier they got, the more beautiful flowers they gave.

Very soon, we started seeing some bees "attacking" the heads of the cucumbers and tomatoes. I thought these bees were about to kill the beautiful flowers, but Daddy told me they would help the male flowers marry the female flowers through something called "pollination," which would help transform the flowers into fruits. Wow! I never knew that flowers also get married!

At this point, Joshua-Enoch asked Daddy, *"How can plants get married if they cannot have a wedding?"* Daddy responded to this funny question by saying that plants have their own way of having weddings, but we human beings just don't know all about it. But by studying how plants pollinate, we can better understand that.

True to Daddy's words, the plants in the garden got married. Some of them became pregnant and were carrying their babies inside their bellies. As for where and how plants carry their babies, we will address those hard and interesting questions in another book. The good thing is that plants don't carry their offspring for 9 months as human beings do.

One day, Daddy noticed that the watermelon, cucumber, and tomato plants had started bearing fruit. Daddy was happy because he knew that very soon these plants would produce fruit for our family. Daddy then called us to show us the Baby fruits. When we came close to Daddy, he announced the news to us, but we could not see the Baby fruits yet. We asked Daddy, "Where were they? Daddy said that the Baby fruits were sleeping in their bed.

"*BED! I never knew Baby fruits slept so much more in a bed!* I shouted. Daddy replied that not only do Baby fruits sleep, but they also sleep in many beds. I told Daddy to show us the Baby fruit and their bed.

Haha, haha, haha! As Daddy was laughing, he told us that Baby fruits like to rest in green beds, which are the leaves in which they hide themselves. Using his hands, Daddy carefully knocked at the door of the bedroom where Baby Tomato and Baby Cucumber were sleeping. As Daddy carefully removed the leaves hiding the Baby fruits, we saw them smiling at us with their green teeth. And after Daddy kindly removed his hands, the Baby fruits closed their door again. We thought they went back to sleep right away, but wait until I tell you the very important thing that these Baby fruits did! Indeed, as Daddy showed us these fruits, we were all excited not only because they looked beautiful, but also because we knew that the watermelon, tomatoes, and cucumber would be very yummy in our tummies. I wanted to eat the fruit right away, even though it was still very small.

Then, Daddy told us that we had to wait until they got a little bigger, more beautiful, and ready to be eaten before we used our kitchen knife to cut them and eat. Little did I know that all the plants were listening to Daddy and that they became concerned when Daddy talked about a knife.

Because Baby Cucumber and Baby Tomato were almost ready, they knew that they might be the first to experience the knife. Therefore, wisely, the cucumber asked Daddy: "*Could you please repeat what you were telling your children that you will do with the knife?*"

"*Great question!*" Baby Tomato added before continuing: "*For me too, I heard what Daddy said about the knife, and I was about to ask the same question as my friend Baby Cucumber to be sure I did not mishear you.*"

Daddy responded: "*As beautiful and handsome as you all the plants in my garden are, I know you will be delicious. Because I knew that my children would enjoy putting you under their teeth, I was excited to let them know how we would cut you with the knife and feast on you,*" Daddy responded to Baby Cucumber and Baby Tomato.

"*Oh no, why will you cut us and eat us?*" Baby Cucumber and Baby Tomato replied to Daddy.

"*We are friends, and enjoy living and growing in your garden. You give us fresh water and good plant food every day. We are happy, and we want to stay friends forever. Friends don't eat friends,*" Baby Cucumber and Baby Tomato responded to Daddy.

"*Why do you want to hurt us and cut us?*" they added as they looked at Daddy, very sad and concerned.

Daddy responded, "*When you grow up and become juicy, I will cut you, and my family and I will eat you,*" Daddy said.

"*Don't hurt us, don't eat us, we want to live*" they replied to Daddy. They begged Daddy not to ever hurt them, but to keep giving them water and plant food and removing every weed around them. Daddy tried to explain to them that vegetables and fruits are grown in a garden so the gardener's family can eat them. But because Baby Cucumber and Baby Tomato were not able to convince Daddy or to make Daddy change his mind and promise to never cut them, Baby Cucumber came out to their rescue. In fact, the conversation between Daddy, Baby Cucumber, and Baby Tomato took so long that Baby Watermelon grew up, vine, and reached where they were.

As Baby Watermelon was getting close to them, Daddy noticed that it was very big, even bigger than Baby Tomato and Baby Cucumber. As Baby Cucumber and Baby Tomato saw Baby Watermelon coming as if it would save them, they told Daddy, "*Do you see our friend Baby Watermelon? It is bigger than us. It is very juicy and sweet, and just one watermelon can be enough to feed all your family. Don't eat us, go cut Baby Watermelon and eat it.*"

Daddy responded to Baby Cucumber and Baby Tomato: "*Oh! You just told me that friends don't hurt friends. How come you can say that Baby Watermelon is your* friend, *yet you are asking me to cut and eat it, while you don't want me to cut and eat you?*"

Knowing that they were in trouble, they responded to Daddy: "*Please forgive us our sins.*"

Daddy responded: "*I forgive your sins, but my teeth and belly will not forgive you, for they are very hungry. If I forgive you and let you go, my teeth and hunger will be sad, for they need to work and* play, *and eating good food like you is what they like.*" Sad and afraid, Baby Tomato and Baby Cucumber told Daddy, "Why don't *you go eat something else and leave us alone?*"

Daddy responded: "*But I grew you in my garden and I cared for you so I can enjoy you, not to let you live forever. Only God can live forever. But beautiful* cucumbers *and tomatoes need to die in the belly of a human being.*"

As Baby Watermelon heard the conversation, he knew that all of them were in trouble. He then secretly told Daddy, "*Daddy, I am too big and it will take many more weeks before I can be fully grown up and be ready for what you are talking about. But Baby Cucumber and Baby Tomato are already ready. Why don't you cut and eat those for now, and we will review my case* later? Baby Watermelon was saying that because he thought that he could grow his vine and run away.

Quickly, Baby Tomato and Baby Cucumber knew the language that Baby Watermelon was speaking. They understood that Baby Watermelon was trying to run and leave them in a big mess, which would send them to die in Daddy's belly. Therefore, Baby Tomato and Baby Cucumber started to cry loudly. Then, they went on their knees to beg Daddy to forgive them and let them live. How come Daddy can work for so many days in his garden, taking care of these plants, and in the end, these plants want to keep eating plant food, drinking water, and seeing Daddy taking care of them, yet they don't want Daddy to eat them? Is that fair? Can anyone do that? Can anyone work in vain just to grow plants that are becoming very juicy and

SECTION 8: CAN YOU BELIEVE THAT DADDY'S TOMATOES AND CUCUMBER TRAVELED TO HEAVEN?

let them leave while that person starves to death? If you want to know what happened to these plants in Daddy's Garden, let's say our garden, keep reading to discover a very funny story!

Science180: The Place Where the Accurate Interpretation of Universe-Creation and Life-Creation Data Matters

38. Why would Cucumber and Tomato prepare their trip to meet God in Heaven–did they really do that?

Because it seemed to Daddy that these vegetables and fruits were not listening but were wasting his time, Daddy told them that God is the one who gave him the authority to grow and eat them. Therefore, Daddy told them that if they could talk to God and ask Him to give Daddy more food, Daddy might let them live forever and not cut them.

"*Good plan,*" Baby Tomato and Baby Cucumber replied. Then, they asked Dad where God is: "*Where can we find God so we can go talk to him?*"

"*In heaven,*" Daddy replied.

"How can we get there?" they asked.

Daddy replied, "*You should know. Didn't you remember when God was telling me in front of you that I should eat you like food?*" Immediately, they remembered where God is and how to reach Him. They asked Daddy to let them go for now and have a meeting with all the other plants in the Garden, and decide how to meet God. Because they were babies, they did not have a lot of money, and they thought that the other plants in the garden could put together some money for them, so they could buy a nice bike or car that they could use to travel the world and meet God!

During their meeting, all the plants in the garden in Daddy's Garden decided to send Baby Cucumber and Baby Tomato to heaven so that, on their behalf, they could beg God to tell Daddy not to eat them.

True to their words and plan, the plants started making arrangements for Baby Cucumber and Baby Tomato to go to Heaven to talk to God. Suddenly, they wondered how far Heaven is, where God is, and how quickly they can get there. They looked around to see if anyone could help them.

Near the meeting place, they saw a very tall Grand pine tree, taller than all the other trees in the garden. The grand pine tree was eating some breakfast at the top and enjoying the Sun, its friend.

Wow! I never knew plants eat breakfast! Hearing that, my siblings and I broke into laughter, for we thought it was strange for the Grand pine tree to be eating, while its friend, the Sun, is beating us with a lot of heat!

Because they could not reach the top of the grand pine tree, they are thinking about how to get there. As they were speaking and looking up to the sky, they saw an eagle passing by. They asked the eagle if it could give them a ride to the top of the grand pine tree.

"*Of course!*" the eagle answered and took them to the top of the grand pine tree before continuing its journey of chasing some animals it can have for its lunch. While on top, the Grand pine tree told Baby Tomato and Baby Cucumber: "*I don't know the way to heaven, but I know the tallest tree in the whole world, which can take you there or at least show you the way.*"

Baby Cucumber and Baby Tomato asked the Grand Pine Tree: "*What is the name of that tree?*"

SECTION 8: CAN YOU BELIEVE THAT DADDY'S TOMATOES AND CUCUMBER TRAVELED TO HEAVEN?

Grand pine tree replied: *"Sequoia is his name, and it lives very far in California in the United States of America."*

"Where is California, and how can we get there?" They asked the grand pine tree.

"I don't really know," the grand pine tree responded. As they were talking, the Sun, Grand pine tree's friend, heard the conversation and informed them that it knows Sequoia and that it, the Sun, is bigger and higher than Sequoia and that it does not know the way to heaven. The Sun told them that the tallest Sequoia tree is about 300 feet tall, and although some Sequoias are more than 3000 years old, none of them have ever reached the Sun yet, and much less the Heaven, which is far away.

Listening to the Sun, Baby Tomato, and Baby Cucumber realized that it would be difficult for them to find anybody on this earth to take them to Heaven. If the Sun, which is very high above all plants and trees, does not know how to get to Heaven, who can know the way then? To get the answer, keep reading!

Science180: The Place Where the Accurate Interpretation of Universe-Creation and Life-Creation Data Matters

39. Angels helping Baby Tomato and Baby Cucumber

Therefore, feeling helpless, they decided to go on their knees and pray to God. As they went on their knees and started praying, a Holy Angel appeared to them and offered to give them a ride to heaven. For, even before they went on their knees, their prayers were heard in Heaven as soon as they thought about it in their heart.

On their journey to Heaven, they saw many angels, including angels Gabriel, Raphael, Ariel, Sophia, Enoch, Michael, and Uriel. Before they reached Heaven, the angel who was guiding them disappeared because not all angels are allowed to go everywhere in the universe. Each angel has its specific place and mission. Some serve God, and others serve human beings. Some angels stay in heaven, and others just stay on Earth, but because they are spiritual beings, we cannot see them with our eyes.

Then, Baby Tomato and Baby Cucumber heard a loud voice speaking to them: "*Welcome to heaven!*

What brought you here?" Angel Michael asked them.

"*We are here to ask God to tell Daddy, who is growing us in his garden, not to eat us, but to let us live forever,*" they answered.

"*What a request!*" Angel Michael replied to them. "*I have not heard this kind of request from any plant before,*" he added. In one voice, all the angels who were witnessing the conversation told them, "*This is a big request that we cannot solve, but only God can solve it. For God has given authority to men to grow and eat plants. If you are asking Daddy not to eat you, only God can create another food for Daddy; otherwise, Daddy and his children will be hungry.*" The angels told Baby Tomato and Baby Cucumber that God does not want anyone to be like Him, and even the Holy Angels don't change God's plan. Otherwise, they can be cast out like Lucifer, who wanted to be like God.

Hearing this, Baby Tomato and Baby Cucumber clarified to the angels that their goal is not to become like God, but to live forever in Daddy's Garden. They then begged the Holy Angels to please let them meet God and present to Him their need.

"*Alright*" Angel Michael replied.

"*Buckle up and let's go! Don't be afraid, because meeting God is not a simple deal but a big deal*" Angel Michael warned them. In the blink of an eye, Baby Tomato and Baby Cucumber saw themselves very close to the place where God lives. Suddenly, a huge thunderclap rolled, and there was a very loud noise, even louder than that of the biggest thunderstorm and earthquake they had ever heard or felt on Earth. Then they began to feel very hot as they drew near God, for God is fire. Immediately, they started sweating. Baby Cucumber got thirsty, while Bay Tomato got hungry. They asked the angel leading them to do something so they would feel better. For this was not a joke but a very big deal.

Instantly, God sent them His grace and cooled them down. God asked Angel Uriel, who was nearby, to change their clothes and put heavenly clothes on them so they wouldn't burn and die in the presence of God. For God's fire is too much. It is hotter than the Sun. Angel Uriel put on a nice jacket of many colors and covered

SECTION 8: CAN YOU BELIEVE THAT DADDY'S TOMATOES AND CUCUMBER TRAVELED TO HEAVEN?

their faces with something colder than the ice on the Earth's North Pole, so their faces wouldn't burn. Angel Uriel then informed them that, in heaven, nobody eats the kind of food they eat on Earth. On Earth, plants eat dirty soil, but in heaven, there is no soil. The streets of heaven are made of gold, and nobody gets tired or lacks anything there. After they changed their clothes, Baby Tomato and Baby Cucumber were finally ready to meet God. Can you guess what happens next?

Science180: The Place Where the Accurate Interpretation of Universe-Creation and Life-Creation Data Matters

40. Baby Tomato and Baby Cucumber meeting with God in Heaven

"*Welcome!*" a loud voice thundered with fire and lightning, and there appeared something like a firework. Some fire fell on Baby Tomato and Baby Cucumber's face, but although they were scared of it, the fire did not burn them. Lightning struck Baby Tomato's legs, but it was not hurt. Near the place where God lives, Baby Tomato and Baby Cucumber saw millions upon millions of angels singing ceaselessly, "Holy Holy Holy".

Then, one Holy Angel told Baby Cucumber and Baby Tomato, "*Don't be afraid. We were just checking to be sure you are really ready to meet God.*" Baby Tomato and Baby Cucumber thought what they had just experienced was truly grand, and they were unsure what to expect next.

Then, a very beautiful gate was opened for them. Everywhere, there were light, gold, beautiful flowers; beautiful animals; and, most importantly, the whole place was beautiful beyond measure. From afar, they saw God sitting on His throne.

They heard a loud voice saying: "*I am God, the Creator of everything everywhere. I am the Boss of the world.*" As God was speaking, the whole place was shaking, and lightning and fire were everywhere. A special green lightning came from the throne of God and high -fived them. At first, Baby Tomato and Baby Cucumber were scared, but in the end, they understood that in heaven, lightning and thunder are everywhere whenever God speaks. Until this point, Baby Tomato and Baby Cucumber had not said anything to God yet.

Surrounded by many angels and covered with a bright light, God told Baby Cucumber and Baby Tomato, "*I heard that you were looking for me. Although I know what you are asking for, I want you to use your own mouth to tell me why you traveled for such a long distance to come see me face-to-face. If I were not merciful, the light and the fire you have seen in Heaven would have already killed you. Your grandparents did not experience this kind of heat before they died in the summer on Earth.*"

Trembling in the presence of God, Baby Tomato started talking and said, "*God Almighty, we love You, and we know You are very good. Thank You for creating us and allowing Daddy to grow us in his garden. We are just a few months old and are babies. We are cute, juicy, sweet, and full of flavor. We love cookies, ice cream, cheese balls, bread, macaroni and cheese, and hot chocolate, and we like to play. We came to see you because there is a man on Earth called Daddy, who planted us in his garden, and after watering us, giving us good plant foods, and pulling weeds away from us for a long time, he now wants to kill and eat us. We asked him to forgive us, but he said that he and his children are hungry and need to eat. We begged Daddy to find something else to eat, but he said NO. He said that only You, God, can create different foods for his family to eat so that he can leave us alone. Dear God, we are here, so please help us. Tell Daddy not to eat us. We are pretty, nice, and smart. We would like to live forever*".

Finally, it was God's to respond to their request: "*To man, certain things are impossible, but to God, all things are possible. I gave a mission to everything I created. It is I, God, who made Daddy the Boss of the Garden. I told Daddy that you will be saved. You will be all right. I gave Daddy permission and power to grow and eat good fruits and vegetables. By eating you, Daddy is obeying me, but by asking Daddy not to eat you, you are making Daddy's life hard. But now that you came all the way from the Earth to Heaven, and you believe that I have the power to forgive and save, I will do something special for you: I will tell Daddy not to eat you, and I will let you grow in the garden forever until you die one day. But I will tell Daddy to eat all other fruits and vegetables, including the other tomatoes and cucumbers in the garden. You will be the boss of all the cucumber and tomato plants in Daddy's Garden, and Daddy will be the Boss of the Garden. When you get home, invite all the garden plants to a meeting and report to them what I said. Do you have any other questions?"* God asked them.

Baby Tomato said *"No"*, but Baby Cucumber raised its hand and asked: *"God Almighty, when I die in Daddy's Garden after he lets me live for a long time, will you raise me from the dead when you come back to Earth some day?"*

God responded: *"I am glad you believe in me and know that I have the power to save and raise people from the dead. Down there on Earth, there are some people who don't believe in me. Yet I love them and want to save them. Go back to the Earth and enjoy your life. I gave Daddy power to save your seeds after you are dead and, every year, to plant you back and take care of your babies or descendants. If any of them will not pray to me or come to me to ask for help as you did, I will tell Daddy to eat them all. Their salvation will be in Daddy's belly. That is why, before you die, remember to teach your children to obey Me, pray to Me, and glorify Me with beautiful flowers and leaves. If they do that, they will live in peace."*

Hearing that, Baby Cucumber and Baby Tomato praised God and thanked Him for His kindness. Before they left, God blessed them and gave them the power to be the most beautiful fruits in Daddy's Garden. After this, God told the very wise and intelligent Angel Sophia and Angel Arielle to take them on their wings and bring them back to Earth. They left Heaven very happy.

41. Baby Tomato and Baby Cucumber returned from Heaven

In the blink of an eye, they returned to Earth. It was night when they returned. When they were in Heaven, there was no day. Therefore, when they were leaving Heaven, they did not know that they would be returning to Earth in the dark.

As soon as Baby Tomato and Baby Cucumber returned to their home in Daddy's Garden, the whole garden was lit up because their faces were still having some of the light from heaven. Looking through the window of his house, Daddy noticed a change in his garden: the whole garden was shining like the Sun, yet it was dark everywhere. Daddy also noticed that Baby Tomato and Baby Cucumber looked prettier this time than ever. Because this never happened before, Daddy knew that these plants might have brought some news back from Heaven.

As Daddy went inside his room to get ready and welcome Baby Tomato and Baby Cucumber back from the garden, he heard a knock at his door. Knock! Knock!

"*Who is there?*" Daddy asked.

"*It is Baby Tomato and Baby Cucumber,*" they replied. Even before Daddy opened the door, they passed through the door and went to sit on the couch, dressed in the beautiful, many-colored clothes that they got from Heaven. As they entered Daddy's house, it started shining like the Sun, and then Daddy's couch became more beautiful.

Coming out of his bedroom, Daddy was surprised to see them sitting on his couch and crossing their legs like Billionaires. Daddy was shocked because, since the beginning of the whole world, no plant has ever sat on a couch or walked on legs.

"*How did you get inside my mansion without a key, and why is my house shining like the Sun?*" Daddy asked them. With one voice, Baby Tomato and Baby Cucumber answered Daddy: "*We just returned from Heaven, where we met God, who was shining brighter than the Sun, and to whom we presented our need. We were able to enter your house without a key because, as part of the gift God gave us, we can now do a few things that most plants cannot do. But we returned from Heaven, and we have been doing miracles in your garden. Also, because we stayed in God's presence for a while, some of the bright light on His face stayed with us. That is why not only are we brightening your house, but also the whole garden,*" Baby Tomato and Baby Cucumber informed Daddy.

"*Wow! You look prettier than before. I can see that nobody meets God and remains the same. What did God tell you?*" Daddy asked them.

Replying, Baby Tomato and Baby Cucumber said: "*We learned a lot, and to make a long story short, God told us to tell you to forgive us and to let us live, but to eat all of the other tomatoes, cucumbers, and any other vegetables and fruits in the Garden. God told us that, normally, you have the right to eat us, but because we came to Heaven to talk to Him, He gave us a special present by letting us be the boss of the Cucumber and Tomato plants in your garden. He told us that you, Daddy, are the boss of the whole Garden.*"

Daddy replied: "*Great! Did you tell that to all the plants in the garden yet?*"

SECTION 8: CAN YOU BELIEVE THAT DADDY'S TOMATOES AND CUCUMBER TRAVELED TO HEAVEN?

"Not yet, we were waiting to talk to you first before we report to them," Baby Cucumber and Baby Tomato answered.

Daddy then told them to go report the news to all the plants in the garden. Upon hearing this, Baby Cucumber and Baby Tomato thanked Daddy for his patience and care. They then decided to go to the conference room, where all the plants were still waiting, playing, listening to music, and dancing to some crazy music. As Baby Cucumber and Baby Tomato approached the meeting place, the other plants waiting for them noticed their new beauty and the light shining on their entire bodies.

"Welcome back," the plants shouted as they saw Baby Cucumber and Baby Tomato ... The plants in Daddy's Garden asked many questions to Baby Cucumber and Baby Tomato. All their questions were answered. But the first thing Baby Cucumber and Baby Tomato told those plants was what God said.

The plants were happy that Baby Cucumber and Baby Tomato went to Heaven and returned safely. But they were sad that Daddy and his children would have to eat all of them except Baby Cucumber and Baby Tomato.

Quickly, they realized that it is better for them to obey God's commandment than to disobey Him. Because they saw how beautiful Baby Cucumber and Baby Tomato were after they returned from Heaven, they wanted to please God so He might take them to Heaven one day. Therefore, all of the plants in Daddy's Garden decided to obey God and let Daddy eat them. At the end, they pray together, raise their hands, and thank God. Then, each of them returned to its home to go to bed.

The news of the important trip that Baby Cucumber and Baby Tomato made spread everywhere, and other plants and even animals heard it and were amazed. Listening to this news of Baby Cucumber and Baby Tomato's meeting with God, many plants that never believed in God now repented and believe. When some plants that were not in Daddy's Garden later heard how Baby Cucumber and Baby Tomato went to heaven and the miracles they performed after their return, they came to believe in God. In other words, the plants in Daddy's Garden converted many other plants to God, and God was very happy because many plants and even people now believe in Him.

After that meeting, all the fruits and vegetables in the garden never argued with Daddy again, but they let Daddy eat them, except Baby Tomato and Baby Cucumber, who visited God in Heaven. That is why, until today, no plant in Daddy's Garden complains anymore. They know that God gave Daddy the power to grow and eat them. The only plants that did not obey properly were the thorns and thistles that grew near Daddy's Garden. Those thorns hurt people who walk by Daddy's Garden. But being smart, Daddy always pulled every weed from his garden and never let any thorn grow there.

A long time after their return from Heaven, Baby Tomato and Baby Cucumber became Mother Tomato and Mother Cucumber. But to their surprise, a few days after their trip to heaven, Baby Cucumber and Baby Tomato realized that the light shining on them was fading, and as time passed, it kept going down until it was completely gone. Little did they know that a few days later, their ability to shine like

123

the sun would be gone! Yet the beauty they received from Heaven remained with them, meaning it never left them, despite their wrinkles from old age.

As Baby Tomato and Baby Cucumber got older, they got many fruits ready to be eaten. But true to God's words, Daddy did not eat any of them, but he ate only the other tomatoes, cucumber, and other fruits in the garden just as God commanded. Baby Tomato and Baby Cucumber were happy that Daddy also respected and obeyed God by not killing or eating them.

Although Daddy kept giving them food and water, Mother Tomato and Mother Cucumber were getting older and older, and one day, they just died, leaving behind many great seeds that fear God like them. Daddy was a little bit sad that these pretty plants finally died. But Daddy was also happy because he had harvested their seeds for future growth.

Because Mother Tomato and Mother Cucumber had so much faith in God and obeyed God's commandment, Daddy loved them so much as well. Daddy put them in his compost bed, knowing that very soon, they would bless the soil with the pretty chemicals in them. From that point forward, all the Tomatoes and Cucumbers that Daddy had been growing in his garden were only seeds from Mother Tomato and Mother Cucumber.

From this story, we learned that God created everything for a reason, and that if each of us plays our role and is kind toward others, we can live better lives and let God govern the universe. We also learned that it is good to ask questions and even to ask God for help. By asking questions, you may get the answer you are looking for.

42. How does God know all the languages in the world?

As we were thinking about the Baby Tomato and Baby Cucumber story, many questions came into our minds. I wondered how they managed to know the language of God. I did not know that plants have a tongue they can use to speak. But I understand that God can speak any language, for He can do anything.

Therefore, as we were around the dining room table, and I was planning to ask Daddy to explain that to me, Joelle-Major jumped in and asked a similar question about creation. Indeed, because God spoke the word during creation and things were created, my sister Joelle-Major asked Daddy the language that God used to create everything.

Daddy began his answer by saying that there are thousands of languages in the world and that most people speak more than one language. For example, although English is the main language for most people in the US, in other countries, most people speak more than one language. Some of these languages include Hebrew, Spanish, German, Portuguese, Russian, and African dialects. For example, Daddy speaks more than 5 languages, including French.

At the beginning of life on Earth, all the people spoke one language, which some think was Hebrew. It was the disobedience of human beings that caused God to create more languages in the world to divide the people and force them not to stay in the same place. For God wanted human beings to move to other places and take advantage of other good things He created in the world. If they just stay in one place, people cannot use all of what God created.

Because God is the creator of all languages, He understands all of them. He knows everything and can do anything. But he does not speak our languages. Hence, during creation, the language God used was not any of the languages human beings speak. The language that God speaks is not something that human beings can speak or understand. For example, God can understand our thoughts, meaning what we are thinking. And thought is a language, yet it has no voice like the sound we make with our mouth. In other words, it is sometimes possible to know what some people are thinking, yet that knowledge or thinking is not something they speak about; it is in their minds. God can speak to us through our dreams, yet we don't know what language we speak in them. In short, not all languages are spoken with the mouth; yet they exist and are real. Therefore, don't be surprised that God can even understand plants when they talk.

43. Why do we wash the vegetables harvested in our garden before eating them?

One day, some fruits, including tomatoes and cucumbers, in the garden were mature enough to be harvested. Using a kitchen knife, Daddy cut them. Joshua-Enoch picked one of them and was about to put it in his mouth right away to eat. I stopped him and told him not to eat it yet, as it has to be washed first.

"But because they are pretty, why do we have to wash them before eating them?" my brother asked me.

Based on what Daddy taught me before, I told him that the fruits in the garden may contain some bacteria, viruses, and other germs that need to be washed off first.

"Bacteria! What does that mean?" he asked.

Daddy looked at me and was waiting to see what I would answer him. I noticed that Daddy was giving me an opportunity to teach my little brother something. Therefore, I taught Joshua-Enoch that when plants and animals were being formed, many other types of living things were also formed. Some of them are very small, so small that our eyes cannot see them. Some of them are very dangerous and can kill. Some of these little living things are called bacteria. Certain things called viruses were also formed, and although they are not really living things, they can cause harm and death.

Some bacteria are good, and some live inside our bellies. After we eat our food, such as the cucumber and tomatoes, the good bacteria in our belly will help to break down the food so our body can easily absorb it and send the good nutrients into our blood. Then, the blood distributes nutrients throughout our body.

As I was speaking, I could see that, quietly, my sister Joelle-Major was soaking everything into her brain, for she was listening carefully, putting her hands on her chin and her elbows on the dining table. When she was a baby, my sister Joelle-Major did not speak a lot, but she thinks a lot. When she was in her Kindergarten and 1st grade, she did not speak much, neither at school, nor at home, but she was the tallest and the smartest of all the students in her class. In fact, she was the only student admitted to the gifted program across all 4 first-grade classes at her school!!

Then, coming back to the question we were addressing, Joshua-Enoch said: "*Wow, I did not know that other things are living inside of my belly. I thought that my body was for me only. I never knew that other beings were there. But because those bacteria won't hurt me, I will not complain*".

Continuing my speech, as Daddy was listening to all of us, I taught my brother and sister that the viruses that could be on the skin of the cucumber and tomato can be dangerous. I was happy that Daddy let me teach my siblings. I liked it when my Daddy let me learn to lead them. That empowered me and helped me to gain more skills. At this point, Daddy intervened to add something to what I was saying:

"*Do you remember Covid-19?*" Daddy asked us.

Joelle-Major replied: "*Oh yes! I will never forget COVID-19. I still remember when it hit.*

SECTION 8: CAN YOU BELIEVE THAT DADDY'S TOMATOES AND CUCUMBER TRAVELED TO HEAVEN?

I was about to start pre-K in 2020 when COVID-19 put the whole world to a stop. Most schools were closed, and people were in quarantine, meaning that people were staying in their homes and not going anywhere, where they could spread the virus. If they had to go anywhere, they had to wear a mask so they wouldn't breathe in the virus. Because it was so bad, I was not able to attend pre-K, but I had to stay home and learn from home. Because I could not attend pre-K, I had to start school in Kindergarten in 2021." After saying this, Joelle-Major leaned back on her chair, her elbow on the dining table, and her hands on her chin! I knew she was ready to take more into her brain!

Daddy then asked me if I had anything else to add.

I then explained to my brother and sister that COVID-19 is a type of virus. Because I didn't want to get sick of any kind of virus or bacteria, I understood that it is very important to wash all vegetables and fruits before eating them, no matter where they come from, our garden, the market, or the store. Therefore, we took all the vegetables to the kitchen so they could be washed with clean water.

Paying close attention to what I was saying, my brother, Joshua-Enoch, asked: *"How many bacteria and viruses are there in the whole universe?"*

Knowing that I may not have the right answer to this big question, Daddy said there are billions upon billions of viruses and that scientists have not yet discovered them all. Some scientists have shown that there are more viruses on Earth than stars in the universe. Just like bacteria, viruses are everywhere on Earth, and we need to be careful so they don't contaminate us, meaning avoid exposing ourselves to them and becoming sick.

After I finished explaining to my brother and sister what bacteria and viruses mean, Daddy told me that he was proud of me not only because I learned what he taught me about creatures, but also because I was able to properly teach my brother and sister. I was happy to hear that and enjoyed teaching my brother and sister what I had learned. I also enjoy drawing things and doing math!

Science180: The Place Where the Accurate Interpretation of Universe-Creation and Life-Creation Data Matters

SECTION 9: HOW ANIMALS WERE FORMED

44. Can you explain how animals were formed without knowing what they are?

The world is filled with many animals. Before explaining how animals were made, I will first show you the pictures of some animals.

Figure 57: Rhinoceros. © 2025 by Nathanael-Israel Israel / www.Israel120.com

Figure 58: Giraffe. © 2025 by Nathanael-Israel Israel / www.Israel120.com

Figure 59: Tiger. © 2025 by Nathanael-Israel Israel / www.Israel120.com

Figure 60: Llama. © 2025 by Nathanael-Israel Israel / www.Israel120.com

Figure 61: Gorilla. © 2025 by Nathanael-Israel Israel / www.Israel120.com

Figure 62: Lion and lioness. © 2025 by Nathanael-Israel Israel / www.Israel120.com

Nathanael-Israel Israel: Author of "Turbulent Origin of Life"

Figure 63: Koala. © 2025 by Nathanael-Israel Israel / www.Israel120.com

Figure 64: Lamb. © 2025 by Nathanael-Israel Israel / www.Israel120.com

Figure 65: Rabbit. © 2025 by Nathanael-Israel Israel / www.Israel120.com

Figure 66: Monkey. © 2025 by Nathanael-Israel Israel / www.Israel120.com

Figure 67: Butterfly. © 2025 by Nathanael-Israel Israel / www.Israel120.com

Figure 68: Flock of birds. © 2025 by Nathanael-Israel Israel /
www.Israel120.com

Figure 69: A bird. © 2025 by Nathanael-Israel Israel / www.Israel120.com

Figure 70: Baby birds. © 2025 by Nathanael-Israel Israel / www.Israel120.com

Figure 71: Peacock. © 2025 by Nathanael-Israel Israel / www.Israel120.com

Figure 72: Duck. © 2025 by Nathanael-Israel Israel / www.Israel120.com

Figure 73: Goldfish. © 2025 by Nathanael-Israel Israel / www.Israel120.com

Figure 74: Cow. © 2025 by Nathanael-Israel Israel / www.Israel120.com

Figure 75: Deer. © 2025 by Nathanael-Israel Israel / www.Israel120.com

Figure 76: Giraffe and ostrich. © 2025 by Nathanael-Israel Israel / www.Israel120.com

Figure 77: Horse. © 2025 by Nathanael-Israel Israel / www.Israel120.com

Figure 78: A nice ruminant. © 2025 by Nathanael-Israel Israel / www.Israel120.com

Figure 79: Squirrel. © 2025 by Nathanael-Israel Israel / www.Israel120.com

Nathanael-Israel Israel: Author of "Turbulent Origin of Life"

Figure 80: Zebra. © 2025 by Nathanael-Israel Israel / www.Israel120.com

Science180: The Accurate and Most Trusted Universe-Origin and Life-Origin Decoder

45. How were animals made?

The Earth is not just filled with plants and human beings. It also contains many animals. Therefore, we cannot explain the formation of the Earth without also explaining how animals were made.

"How did God make animals?" Joelle-Major asked Daddy. In response, Daddy said that there are millions of animals in the world. Some are mammals (meaning they have breasts, like humans or cattle), others are fish, birds, reptiles (such as snakes), or insects.

Some animals are very small, while others are very big. Some are friendly, others are not. For example, crickets are small, while dinosaurs and elephants are big. Some animals, like sheep, are nice, while others, like alligators and lions, are mean.

Herbivores are animals that eat grass, while carnivores eat meat. Some animals are clean, while others are unclean. No matter what they look like, all animals were formed by God using soil and water. To form them, God first thought about what they would look like, and then He made it happen. Just as an egg can grow from being small to becoming a perfect adult body, so also, before animals were born, something like a seed started moving on Earth. That thing went through changes, gained form and functions, and became an animal. Daddy told us that as we grow older and learn more things in school, like biology and chemistry, he will explain in more detail how all the body parts of animals were formed. But those who are adults and want to know more can check out the books that Daddy wrote on the origin of life at www.Science180.com/life.

Then, I asked Daddy: *"What large creature did God create, and how many are there?"*

Responding, Daddy said that God formed many large creatures on the land and in the waters. In the waters, some of those big creatures were dolphins, sharks, sea lions, whales, and many big fish. On the land, the largest creatures were dinosaurs, elephants, giraffes, rhinoceroses, hippopotamus, cows, bears, moose, buffaloes, and many more. Some animals, like dinosaurs, have already disappeared, and some will disappear very soon. The largest animal in the world is the blue whale; it can reach almost 100 feet, or more than 30 meters. The biggest land animal is the elephant. No matter how big or small they are, all animals were formed using soil and water.

46. Do all animals obey God?

Did you ever wonder whether all animals obey God? If you have ever asked that question, know that you are not alone. I, too, have asked Daddy that same question: *"When the animals were formed, did they obey God's instructions?"*

Indeed, because I learned that human beings do not always obey God, I asked Daddy whether animals do the same or always obey God's commandments. Daddy replied that God planned for everything He created to obey Him, but He did not force anything or anyone to obey Him.

The Bible details how God wants people to live. But the Bible did not say much about the commandments that God gave to animals. Before Adam and Eve sinned, animals were obeying God. They even went to Adam so he could name them. After Adam and Eve sinned, some animals started disobeying them.

Some books written by Jews who lived more than 2000 years ago showed that animals used to communicate with human beings, but that conversation stopped the day Adam and Eve sinned. Because demons (a name given to bad spirits) could have also entered some animals, just like they enter some human beings all the time, it is possible that some demons have entered some animals and are making them disobey God. Therefore, we cannot say for sure that all animals are obeying God's instructions today. But, at one point in the past, we know that they did. What matters for us is not to know how or if animals obey God or not, but to obey God ourselves, even if everybody or everything else in the world chooses to disobey Him. Those who obey God will be rewarded one day.

47. Did God create any bad animals that can hurt people?

I enjoyed going to the zoo with my parents. At the zoo, I saw many animals. Some were friendly, and others were not. My favorite animals are giraffes and lambs. I even have toys of them. I don't like snakes, for they can kill people. Today, although there are many cool animals, the world is filled with animals that can hurt. Some animals destroy, while others are nice, and people play with them.

- But who created the bad animals?
- Was it God?
- If yes, how can God, who is good, create bad animals?
- Were bad animals present when Adam and Eve were in the Garden of Eden?

When Daddy was teaching us about creation, I wondered if God created any bad animals that could have hurt Adam and Eve. As I asked this question, Daddy told me that God is a good God and He never created anything bad. But some of the things He created refused to obey Him, and therefore they made themselves bad. In other words, certain creatures have the ability to change themselves from being good to becoming bad. Even demons were originally created holy. However, from the moment they refused to obey God, they became bad. To this day, many angels called holy angels still obey God. They could have chosen to disobey God as Lucifer did, but they chose to obey God's commandments.

No animal in the Garden of Eden was able to hurt Adam and Eve. Don't forget that, before he disobeyed God, Adam was the boss of everything God created on Earth. It was after Adam and Eve sinned that some animals may have tried to hurt them.

As of today, some animals may be disobeying God. This may explain why some animals are called clean animals, while others are called unclean animals. It is not that the clean animals go to the store to buy nice clothes to put on, or that they go to a washing machine to wash those clothes, so they stay clean all the time. It is not that unclean animals never shower, or that they smell all the time, or that they don't have beautiful clothes. The truth is that all animals have beautiful skin colors, but there is something in them, like a spiritual thing or a mindset, that makes some clean and others unclean. That is why God forbade those who believe in Him from eating certain animals. For instance, although many people like pigs, the Bible said that they are dirty. Even if you wash them and put a nice necklace on their necks or dress them in beautiful white clothes, pigs will prefer the mud and return straight into the dirt. Yet, some people enjoy eating pork, but others don't. In the same way, some animals, such as lions and other carnivores, enjoy eating other animals. Even if a deer prays to a lion so the lion will not kill and eat it, the lion will not listen and will still kill and eat it. An animal like a sheep, or a lamb, is not aggressive. Although some people don't like their smell, the Bible said that they are clean and can be eaten. In other words, animals have different natures, and, because we don't know their history, we cannot say for sure why they behave in certain ways or whether they are obeying God or not. Even if we know that does not matter as much as we work on our attitudes so we can live a great life that honors God, our Creator.

.

Nathanael-Israel Israel: Author of "Turbulent Origin of Life"

SECTION 10: HOW HUMAN BEINGS WERE FORMED

48. How were people made and where do babies come from?

Where do human beings come from? How did we get here? Those are questions everybody wants to know. In her own style, my sister Joelle-Major asked Daddy: *"How did God make people?"* To respond, Daddy told us that the Earth is filled with more than 8 billion human beings. Some live in Africa, others in America, Europe, Asia, and Australia. They have certain things in common and other things not in common. Although some people are black and others are white, they are the same and unique. For instance, every human being has red blood. Nobody has white blood or black blood. On the inside, people are pink. Some people speak English, others speak French, Spanish, and many more languages.

All those human beings descended from Adam and Eve, who were the first people that God created. Adam was created before Eve. Then, they began having babies, who, in their turn, grew up, got married, and had their own babies. Those babies grew up and also had their own babies, and small, small, the world was filled with people. In other words, the more kids they had, the more the world was filled with human beings. But let's not forget that, as more babies were being born, many adults were dying. Because the number of babies born is higher than the number of people who die, the number of people in the end keeps growing on Earth. As of 2025, there are more than 8 billion human beings on Earth.

Today, God is no longer making people, but people get married and have children. In response to that statement, I asked Daddy, *"Did babies just pop up in the belly?"*

Everybody in the room laughed at that silly question as Daddy was typing everything we were saying very fast. By the way, Daddy types very fast like a robot. To answer my question, Dad said that how babies are born is a miracle. When people get married and become husband and wife, they start sleeping together in the same room. Then, a miracle happens for them, and a baby starts growing in the mother's belly. God is a God of miracles! The baby stays in the mommy's womb for about 9 months. As the baby grows in the belly, Mommy's belly gets bigger. When the baby is born, it is very small, and the parents take care of it until it is old enough to go to school, usually around 4-5 years of age.

When they are small, babies cannot take care of themselves. They poop and pee in diapers. They cry too much, put food on their face, play a lot, make a lot of mess, and have to learn a lot of things before they can become adults one day, and maybe get married after finishing school and having a job, meaning making enough money to take care of themselves and their own children. Some people choose to stay single, meaning they don't get married.

As Daddy was talking, Joshua-Enoch raised his hand and asked: *"How did Eve come out of Adam, but today boys are not able to give birth to people, but only girls?"* Daddy told him that he was thinking too much. First of all, little girls cannot give birth to people, but only adult women. When a woman is pregnant, the baby can be heavy to carry, and little children cannot carry babies yet. Also, little children don't have the money to take care of a baby. Also, their bodies are not ready to have a baby yet. Everything in life has its own season. A time to be a baby and a time to become an adult who can have a baby. Babies play with baby toys, study to become very smart, obey their parents, go to school, do their homework, clean at home, behave well, listen to parents, respect people, stay organized, and display other good attitudes that will make them good people.

Going back to Joshua-Enoch's question, Daddy said that Adam did not give birth to Eve, but God used Adam's rib to form Eve. In other words, Adam was never pregnant with Eve or with anybody else. Men don't get pregnant, but only women do. It was not that Adam had a piece of Eve's body inside of him. It was a miracle God did by using a rib or bone of Adam to form Eve.

Today, human beings are formed from an egg that God miraculously places in a woman's belly after she is married and lives with her husband. Although some women can get pregnant before getting married, it is better for them to grow up first, go to school, have a job, and ensure they are mature and that they or their husband have enough money to support their children before having one.

As Daddy was finishing answering this question asked by Joshua-Enoch, another one popped in my head: "*Where does the egg have to stay when there is a lot of stuff inside the mom's belly?*" I asked.

Daddy said that my question is important and great. He told us that, although there are many things in people's bellies, each thing has its own place. There is a place for the food we eat in our mouths to go, like the stomach and the intestines, until we poop it out or take some nutrients into our blood. There is also a place for the egg that becomes a baby to stay in the belly until it grows and is born. Each thing has its place, and some of those places are difficult to explain, particularly to children who cannot or who are not meant to understand certain things yet. Daddy told us that as we grow, we will know where babies stay in the womb and how they get there. He also told us that all babies start with a tiny egg, smaller than a grain of sand on the seashore, which we cannot see with our eyes, but it grows very fast until it becomes a baby ready to be born.

A woman's belly and a man's belly are different. They have certain things in common and other things that are different. That is why men cannot become pregnant, but only women. Also, babies cannot become pregnant yet, but they have to grow until they become adults first before they can be able to bear a baby.

But remembering what I read in the Bible's Book of Genesis, I did not understand how God made Adam from the dust of the ground. Therefore, to be sure, I asked Dad: "*How did God create people from soil?*"

When God was creating people, He indeed used the soil. But first, He thought about what He wants human beings to look like. Just as a carpenter can use wood and shape things, or just as a builder can use the soil or cement to build a house, so also God used the soil and water to make people. God is powerful and can do anything. Although God used the soil to make people, no human being today can use soil to make anyone. For God put His spirit in human beings so that they can function like God in certain things they do. We cannot see spirits with our eyes, but they are real. Human beings have certain invisible things in them (which we cannot see), but which wild animals don't have. That is why human beings think differently, worship and praise God, pray to God, and do things that animals and plants cannot. All human beings are different because God created each of us to be unique. That is why it is also important for us not to compare ourselves to others or try to become someone else. It is better to focus on who we are and what we have, and live our lives the best we can to honor God and help others.

49. How were bones made, and why do birds fly but people cannot?

Joelle-Major was interested in knowing how bones were made. Therefore, Daddy taught us that bones are the hard parts of our bodies that allow us to stand up. Without bones, we could not walk, and we would be squishy like Jello. Even most animals have bones. Sheep, chickens, cows, goats, bony fish, and other animals have bones. Animals that have bones in their bodies are called vertebrates. Animals that lack bones are called invertebrates. Animals like insects and worms do not have bones.

Bones are parts of the things that were formed during the creation of life. Bones are very hard because they are made of strong chemicals. An example of these chemicals is calcium, which is also found in teeth. Hence, teeth are also very hard. Calcium is abundantly found in foods such as milk, and it helps make bones strong. If human beings didn't have bones, they could not stand, jump, or do handstands, and life could have been very difficult. Hence, we need to be grateful for having calcium in our bones.

Although plants don't have bones, some have very strong stems that allow them to stand upright. For trees, the main stem is called the trunk. Plants that lack a strong stem end up vining on the ground like sweet potato, cucumber, and watermelon plants. Two of the chemicals that make plants strong or rigid are lignin and cellulose. Some of them are made of sugar, tightly wrapped.

Because Daddy has given us the chance to ask any question that we have concerning the creation of anything in nature, I came up with a very important question. Do you want to hear what it is? If you answered yes, here it is: *"Why do birds fly but people cannot?"*

In fact, I always wanted to fly like angels. I have spent a lot of hours drawing pictures of angels. All that is because I love angels. Here, by angels, I mean holy angels, not the fallen angels who disobeyed God. I remember having asked Daddy many times to pray to God so He would let me fly. Usually, when I talk like that, Daddy likes my faith and prays with me. But my prayers are not answered yet, for I have never flown yet. Therefore, as Daddy was teaching us about creation, I asked him why birds fly but people cannot.

Daddy replied that birds fly because of how they were made and how their bodies function or work in the air. Birds are not as heavy as human beings. Most birds are lighter than human babies. In other words, even human babies are heavier than most birds. The heavier a bird, the more difficult it is for it to fly. That is why the ostrich, which is the heaviest bird, runs very fast but cannot fly.

Birds were also made to have a shape that eases their flight. That is why airplanes are designed to look like birds. For instance, airplanes have wings and tails like birds. Although airplanes are very heavy, even heavier than the heaviest birds, they fly because they have a big machine that blows air in a certain way that helps them fly. When birds fly, they flap their wings and move the air. Human beings don't have wings or feathers. Although we have arms and can flap them, it is not enough for us to move the air and fly.

Although we can jump high on a trampoline, we cannot fly, for gravity pulls us back to the Earth. If gravity were not there to pull us back to the Earth, we might just be floating in the air. For this reason, astronauts who go into space, like the International Space Station, float. Although people cannot fly, they can run, jump, and even invent things like big airplanes or jets that fly faster than the fastest birds. In other words, God did not allow us to fly with wings, but He gave us a big brain to think and invent airplanes we can use to fly.

Finally, it is important to mention that angels fly despite being very huge. It is all about God's design. Daddy also taught me that, for now, it is important to be content with what I have, including the ability to walk or run, rather than wanting to fly like angels. Who knows if, when flying like an angel, I may go to places not fit or good for me to live in, or get lost in the sky? For example, if people try to fly to the Sun, they may not get there before the Sun fries them. Because I want to be alive, I think for now, I will not complain even if I cannot fly yet. I thank God I can jump on the trampoline.

50. Why are human beings the "boss" of all creatures on Earth?

Do you know that, in the beginning, Adam was the Boss of every creature on Earth? Oh Yes? He was. Indeed, the Bible said that God gave Adam the power to dominate the Earth. Something happened, and Adam could no longer lead everything on Earth. Because I did not know why, I asked Daddy the following question: "Why did God let Adam be the boss of what God created on Earth?"

Daddy told me that God's plan was for Adam to lead everything on Earth. Because God created many living and nonliving things, He organized them according to specific laws or instructions. Because it is not good to have two captains in the same boat, God decided to make Adam the Boss of everything on Earth. This means that every creature on Earth was supposed to obey Adam's commandment if Adam himself could obey God. But because Adam and Eve sinned, the authority that God gave Adam over the other creatures was lost. Therefore, everything on Earth does not obey Adam anymore. In the end, some animals, such as snakes, have been killing people. But some animals that the Bible calls clean animals may still be obeying God. If not, why would God tell people not to eat unclean animals but clean animals only?

Although Adam sinned, and certain things on Earth are not going or behaving as God initially planned, human beings are still the most dominant beings on Earth. For example, no animal or plant is as smart or as powerful as human beings. To make a long story short, as of today, human beings are no longer the boss of everything God created on Earth, as it should have been if they had not disobeyed and kept disobeying God. That is why it is important that we believe in God and obey Him so that He forgives and saves us.

51. How did the first human beings look after they were formed?

As Daddy was answering our questions, each time we addressed a question, we wanted to know who asked it. We liked having our name mentioned for the one who asked the big and very important questions that the children across the whole world will enjoy. The question we are going to address now was asked by me, Josephine.

Daddy taught us that, when Adam was created, he looked like a human being with supernatural skills. In the beginning, Adam was holy, meaning he had no sin in him. In those days, He could clearly see angels singing and praising God in heaven. His body was filled with fire, and he was very powerful. All animals respected him, and he gave them commandments, and they obeyed. Adam had many skills and gifts that most people don't have today. In the days of Adam, people lived for hundreds of years. For example, Adam died at the age of 930 years.

Although Adam was holy and perfect in the beginning, he did not know many things that most people know today. For instance, it was long after Adam died that science was created. Adam did not go to school. Because he was the first human being, there was no person to be his teacher. Not only did Adam not go to school, but he was also alone for a while before God made Eve to become his wife. Then, they got children who could give him company. Eve, who was the second human being, did not know better than Adam. But Adam and Eve learned a lot of things from God. In fact, what God wanted from them was not even to learn many things as students do today, but to obey God so God could provide for all their needs. Today, people go to school and learn a lot, but unfortunately, some of what we learn from our teachers is wrong. If we obey God, there are certain things we don't need to learn before all our needs are met.

In the beginning, God used to talk to Adam face-to-face. But things changed when Adam and Eve disobeyed God and listened to Satan, who used to be called Lucifer before being chased away from his initial place after he tried to become like God. After Adam and Eve ate the forbidden fruit, problems started to occur on Earth. Therefore, Adam had to sweat and work very hard before he could eat. But we cannot blame Adam for all the problems in the world today. In fact, some people think that if Adam had not sinned, there would not be any problem in the world today, there would not be any sickness, hunger, thirst, hard work, a need to go to school, or to do homework, a need to work hard most time, a need to sleep just for 8 hours instead of 24 hours a day or 20 hours a day like a lion, a need to learn to do math, reading, or any STEAM stuff, a need to clean the house or to do dishes every day, etc. To make a long story short, some people put all the problems in the world on the head of Adam as if he caused them all. But it is not correct to blame Adam or Eve for all our problems. For we too have a chance to obey God all the time, but usually we don't.

Praise be to God that when we do bad things sometimes and ask Him to forgive us, He always forgives and gives us a fresh start. We thank God for his mercy, and we will obey Him so He can be happy with us! It is also a mistake to think that God is the source of all the problems in the world. People are also causing problems, and the world is also getting old, and things are getting complicated. Not because there is a God will we think that no problem should exist in the world. In other words, it is very wrong to think that there is no God because the world has problems that are not solved yet. In fact, God created a great and beautiful world, but people and demons have been doing bad things, which have been making life on Earth miserable. For that reason and others, we cannot blame God for our problems.

Even if we believe in God, there will still be problems in this world and in life. For this world is not made to be free of problems. Wherever there are human beings in this universe, there will be problems. Even if Adam and Eve had not sinned, there may still be problems on Earth today, for other human beings after them could have caused trouble. The only way to avoid problems is to obey God 100%, which is not easy in this life filled with problems almost everywhere. Hence, God does not expect us to be 100% perfect before He loves and saves us. Our job is to believe in God and properly handle or address the problems that come our way. We also need to learn how to ask God to help us every day until we are with Him forever in Heaven, the only place in the whole universe where there is no problem. Hence, we can't wait to go to Heaven one day and leave behind the problems in this world. Meanwhile, let us learn from our parents and live a good life that adds fewer problems to the many problems already present in the world.

My last question about the formation of human beings was how the universe and God himself existed before God created Adam and Eve. I wish there were a movie or recording about that event. I would just sit and watch it entirely while eating some popcorn, cake, and drinking some apple juice. Daddy told me that Adam and Eve were the last living things that God created. Before creating Adam, God created plants, cattle, fish, birds, reptiles, insects, lions, cheetahs, gorillas, giraffes, and many more animals. According to the Bible, plants were formed on the 3rd day of creation, while all animals were created on the 4th, 5th, and 6th day. Adam was created on the 6th day, and then God rested on the 7th day. In fact, Daddy taught us that Adam was created on a Friday in the first month of the Jewish civil calendar, meaning around September and October. And this happened about 6000 years ago.

Because God never changed, He is the same yesterday, today, tomorrow, and forever. In other words, He is the same even before He started creation. The only difference is that before the creation of the very first human beings, God was alone. The first beings that God created were angels. After creation, God is surrounded by all His creatures. He lives far above the universe He created, and we cannot see Him with our eyes. Yet, we believe He exists. One day, those who believe in Him will see Him face to face and live with Him forever and ever. Amen!

Nathanael-Israel Israel: Author of "How Baby Universe Was Born"

SECTION 11: IMPORTANT FUNNY QUESTIONS ABOUT HOMES AND TOYS

52. Other important children's questions we cannot ignore

During our conversations with Daddy, we asked many questions that are not directly related to the formation of the universe, but to the formation of very important things on Earth, such as houses, televisions, doors, toys, cars, balls, and hats. Although these questions may not seem important for adults, for us, children, they were very important to know:

- How did God make houses?
- How did God make the television that we watch?
- How did God make the doors of houses?
- How did God make toys?
- How did God make cars like my toy Hot Wheels cars?
- How did God make the balls that we play with?
- How did God make cool hats that some people put on their heads?

If you want to know the answer to these important questions, please keep reading. After we solve the problems that trouble many children, we will end this book with other major questions, such as the age of God, the age of the Earth, and the age of the whole universe. As you can see, many important things are coming up very soon. For now, let's first talk about children's stuff!

Ready? Let's go!

Nathanael-Israel Israel: Acknowledged as Undisputable Specialist of All Questions at the Intersection of Science and Biblical Creation

53. Did God make houses?

Joelle-Major and Joshua-Enoch needed Daddy to talk to us more about how God made homes. Daddy told us that God does not make houses today. People build houses. Some houses are very nice, and others are not. People build houses according to how much money they have. Some people cannot afford to build houses, so they rent, meaning they pay the owner every month so the owner can let them live in the house. Some people called homeless don't have a home because they cannot afford to buy or rent an apartment or a home.

To build houses, people use different materials like soil, brick, water, concrete, wood, and iron. They also use different tools. We like to play and build toy houses. Sometimes we even built houses out of mud. To do that, Daddy let us dig a small hole in our backyard, gather some soil, and mix it with water. Then, we planned what to build as we went. We don't really have a big design like adults do, but we just play with the mud and have a lot of fun!

Daddy told us that God had a plan before He built everything in nature. I asked Daddy whether God built a house for the first human beings He created or not. Daddy answered that God indeed built a home for the first human beings on Earth: Adam and Eve. Called the Garden of Eden, that home was better than the best and nicest mansion on Earth today. It did not take too long before Adam and Eve were chased away from that nice place. Since then, people have been building various types of houses. Even wild animals build their own small house. Some birds like to build nests too. Some animals like to dig in the ground and make a hole where they can hide. Some animals, like fish that live in water, don't really build houses. They just swim and change places, and sometimes build nests to lay their eggs so that they can have babies. Animals that have a house usually come back to their house very often to rest and sleep. Sometimes, birds have to fly thousands of miles just to escape bad weather, such as winter. But when the nice weather returns, most animals like to also return to their homes.

After saying this, Daddy reminded us that God is building houses in Heaven for people who believe in Him. So that God can be happy and make our heavenly houses nicer, we need to behave very well and believe in Him. We thank God for the nice house that my parents own in the USA. Although God does not create houses for people today, it is important to know that the whole Earth is like a nice house for human beings to live in. For example, if the Earth were as hot as a stove or as cold as a freezer, life would have been very difficult. That is why we thank God for what we have, and we also need to help the homeless who have no home. My siblings and I enjoy riding in our family's car with our parents to help some homeless people with some money and food. Particularly, my brother Joshua-Enoch said that when he grows up, he wants to be a medical doctor and a prophet so he can help people, the homeless, the widows, the refugees, the orphans, and all kinds of needy people. What a big, nice dream!

54. Did God make TVs, and what shows does He watch?

How did God make TVs? Joshua-Enoch asked. Dad answered that God did not make TVs; human beings invented them so they could watch movies, news, shows, etc. God does not need to watch TV shows. As Daddy was talking, my sister Joelle-Major said, "People watch television on TV." I then corrected her by saying that TV is a nickname for television, and that we don't watch TV on television.

Daddy then asked Joelle-Major whether she should keep her remark or answer *(people watch television)* in the book. Joelle-Major replied: *"Keep it!"*

Daddy asked her: *"Why should I keep it?"*

Joelle-Major replied that she wants Daddy to keep her remark because it is silly, and she likes that part. Hearing that frank or honest suggestion, we all laughed and agreed to keep it so that when we grow up and read this book, we can remember some of the silly things we said when we were young. We are proud to be answering questions as best as we can, and there is nothing to be ashamed of, even when we look back when we get old!

We all laughed, and Daddy said he would put all of those questions toward the end of the book in a chapter that he would call *"Silly kids' questions about creation."* Joshua-Enoch jumped into the conversation by saying that Daddy should call that chapter *"Nonsense questions."*

Daddy replied: *"They are not nonsense but they are just kids' questions. For no question is nonsense. It is always better to ask any question you have than not asking because you think it is nonsense."* It is better to ask questions than guess answers and do things wrong, when you could have done it better by asking a question and getting a good answer. That is why we always ask every question we have to Daddy and he answers them all. Very often, Daddy also teaches us about critical things that some parents don't teach their children. All this makes us very special and smart kids who do very well both at home and at school!

Nathanael-Israel Israel: Acknowledged as Undisputable Specialist of All Questions at the Intersection of Science and Biblical Creation

55. Did God make doors?

We enjoy playing in our backyard and listening to loud music. When Daddy lets us play in our backyard, my sister, my brother, and I sometimes like building toy houses after mixing soil with water, even though it can stain our clothes. We usually asked Daddy to let us dig the soil using a small shovel, and each time, he told us to dig a fresh hole, for he did not want us to be digging at the same place, and some scorpions and other animals could be hiding in the soil and bite us as we put our fingers into things. After we were done playing, our Daddy always helped us to close the holes and compact the soil so no animal could go there.

One day, as we were sitting around the dining table listening to Daddy teach us about creation, one of us asked Daddy about how God created doors. Can you guess the name of the person who asked that question? That was my brother Joshua-Enoch.

Daddy responded that God did not make doors that people use on their houses, but He made the trees and the metals that people like carpenters use to make doors. People put doors on their homes so others don't enter them and steal or hurt anybody. Doors help houses to stay cool in the summer and warm in the winter. Doors help prevent animals, including bugs, from entering houses. However, in some countries, people don't even put a door on their house. This is because those people either don't need a door or don't have the money to buy or make one.

Unfortunately, when houses don't have doors, animals, including snakes, rats, birds, raccoons, and bears, can enter a home. People who don't have air conditioning in their homes enjoy opening their doors to get fresh air when they are home. But for safety reasons, it is better to keep the door closed. Even if the doors are closed, snakes and other animals, such as mice, ants, and cockroaches, can try to enter the house.

As an example, Daddy recounted to us a true story when a snake entered his room and went to lie on top of his pot containing cooked beans. It was like the snake smelled the beans and wanted to eat some. Therefore, it entered the room, although Daddy had a door that was closed.

Finally, talking about doors, Daddy stated that God also has a door to heaven. The Bible teaches that Jesus is the way and the door to Heaven.

161
Science180: The Only One Formula Accurate Enough to Explain the
Creation of the Universe and Life

56. Did God make toys?

As you know by now, we love toys. Therefore, you should not be surprised that Joshua-Enoch wanted to know how God made toys.

My brother thought that God was spending His precious time in Heaven to make toys for children. To my brother's surprise, Daddy said, and I know that would be the answer, that God did not make toys, but people make toys for their children to play with. I did not know whether God made toys for Adam and Eve, but what I know is that making toys is not a very big deal for God to do for us before we can play. Even children can make toys.

Sometimes we made toys out of cardboard boxes. We pretended it was a store where we could sell pizza we made with mud, grass, leaves, and seeds that looked like spices. Although we never ate those toy pizzas, Daddy always encouraged us when we displayed some creativity. Daddy would look at them and say they look very delicious! Then, we just pretended and gave them to the bugs outside to eat. However, in real life, we love pizza and ice cream. Do you?

57. Did God make cars?

Almost everybody in our house loves pretty Hot Wheels. Our brother likes funny-looking toy cars. Before Daddy answered Joshua-Enoch's question about how God made cars, Daddy asked us if any of us wanted to answer that question. I said "Me". Then I answered that "People make cars and use them to go to places faster." Daddy added that God does not need a car or an airplane.

God can go anywhere in the whole universe in the blink of an eye. In fact, God does not need to move to any place before he knows everything about that place. God knows everything. People use metals, woods, and electrical components to build cars. And all of those have been created by God.

58. Did God make the balls that we play with?

My sister Joelle-Major answered the question that Joshua-Enoch asked: *"God did not make balls. People made them."* I added that God did not make all the things we see in stores; people made most of them, except for the plants, animals, and people.

To make balls, people use different materials and shape them as they wish. That is the case for soccer balls, basketballs, volleyballs, footballs, etc.

At his turn, Daddy added that God made the planets to look like big soccer balls or basketballs. Holding a ball of yarn in her hand, my sister Joelle-Major asked: *"Are they like this?"*

Daddy replied, *"They have a similar shape* but *are millions of times bigger."* In other words, planets are spherical, meaning they look like huge orange balls.

Nathanael-Israel Israel: Acknowledged as Undisputable Specialist of All
Questions at the Intersection of Science and Biblical Creation

59. Did God make hats so the Sun does not beat down on us?

Daddy has many hats. As Joshua-Enoch is growing, Daddy has been giving him some of those hats. Joshua-Enoch enjoys wearing them. His love for hats was why he wanted to know how God made them. Daddy responded that God did not make hats. People make hats to protect their heads when it is hot or raining. Some people enjoy wearing a hat to look nice or for fashion. Some people put on hats to hide their hair or their lack of hair, or to protect their skin from the Sun.

Some people like to stay beneath trees to cool down when it is too hot. Some people who don't have much money cannot afford to have air conditioning in their rooms. Therefore, they rely on the cool breeze (or wind) and the shade of trees to cool them down when hats cannot do the job. We thank God for our hair, which also helps protect our heads from the Sun, the cold, and other hazards when left unprotected. With this answer, let's turn to more important questions about the age of certain things in the whole world!

Nathanael-Israel Israel: Acknowledged as Undisputable Specialist of All
Questions at the Intersection of Science and Biblical Creation

SECTION 12: HOW OLD IS GOD, THE EARTH, AND THE UNIVERSE?

60. How old is the Earth?

Just like a baby, the Earth was also born on a certain day, a long time ago. Earlier in this book, we did some cool science that proved the dates the Bible gave for the birth of the Earth, the Moon, and the Sun perfectly match the scientific data collected by top scientists over the years. Since creation, the Earth and everything else in the whole universe have grown and are getting older. In other words, many things have changed since the beginning. Certain things have also happened since creation.

People have tried to calculate (which means to find out) the date that the Earth was born, but it is not easy to know. For the Earth was created a long time ago, and no human being was there to see it. However, we can use some things to estimate the date.

Many books have been written about creation. Some are wrong, and others are right. For example, the Bible says the formation of the Earth was finished on the 3rd day of creation, and many things have happened since then. When Daddy put together the time that has passed based on the events that have occurred since creation, he discovered how long it may have taken or how many years have passed. While some people think the universe is millions of years old, Daddy has done a lot of science and told me it's almost 6,000 years old. He figured it out by considering the history of the human beings who lived on Earth before us.

Nathanael-Israel Israel: Author of "Science180 Accurate Scientific Proof of God"

61. How old is God?

Don't you think it would be cool to know the exact date God was born and how old He is? That is what we will figure out now.

Indeed, my sister Joelle-Major is a thinker and is very organized. She likes to help people, and even at school she helps her teachers to clean the classroom. Sometimes, she asked very hard questions. When we were learning from Daddy, she wanted to know God's age. In response, our Daddy told her that such a question is very hard and that even most grown-up people cannot properly understand it. This is because we don't know when God was born. We don't even know if He was ever born. He may always have existed and not needed to be born.

We estimate people's ages by guessing how much time has passed since they were born. We celebrate birthdays when we know the date of birth. But because we don't know the date of God's birth, we cannot celebrate His birthday or calculate His age. Truth be told, I believe that God always existed, and I don't need to know His age before I believe in Him, love Him, live for Him, obey Him, serve Him, be a good child, and do well so I can please Him. That is why, to make a long story short, Daddy said that God is eternal, meaning He always existed and always will exist, forever and ever. And we all said "AMEN!"

"But what about Christmas, which people celebrate as Jesus' birthday?" I asked. Daddy responded that although some people think that Jesus was born on December 25th, meaning on Christmas, the Jews who know Jesus very well believe that He was not born on Christmas, but in the fall on a feast day, which is believed to be the date that God created Adam. That date is around September and October. In other words, Jesus was not born in December but around September or October. By the way, Jesus was born in Israel and lived for about 33 years before He died, rose again on the 3rd day, and went to heaven.

People who believe in Jesus are waiting for Him to return and take them to Heaven so they can be with Him forever and ever. Although Jesus was born about 2000 years ago, it is important to know that He existed before that day. This means that Christmas is not really the birthdate of God, but a date we just celebrate with the world. Some people who don't even believe in Jesus also celebrate Christmas. What matters is not just to celebrate Christmas, but to be sure that we know and believe in Jesus and are saved. Otherwise, those who don't believe in Jesus, but celebrate Christmas, will be shocked one day if they die without believing and confessing Jesus as their Lord and Savior.

I am glad I know Jesus, the Creator of the Universe, and I believe in Him. Everybody in my family also believes in God. We read the Bible and pray to God every day. Every morning, before we get out of bed and brush our teeth, we do our morning devotion (a daily reading that teaches us about God).

Because I am the oldest child, Daddy taught me how to read the Bible first. As I am growing up and know how to read, I don't wait for Daddy in the morning anymore before I read and pray. In fact, I led my siblings to study God's word in the

169

morning. As my sister Joelle-Major is growing, able to read, and learning more sight words, Daddy asked me to teach her how to read our morning devotional. Therefore, since she passed to 2nd grade, she started reading the morning devotional and leading some of our prayers in our bedroom before we came out. Daddy is proud of us for how well we like to read and learn about God.

Although Daddy let us read and pray from a children's daily devotional, he spent a lot of time every day teaching us about God and praying for and with us, including in the morning. He usually comes into our room to listen to us when we pray to God and read in the morning. He also participates with us. He told us that his goal is not to pray with us and for us all the time, but to teach us how to have a relationship with God and to talk to God as he, Daddy, does. Like he always told us, if we learn to walk with God now that we are children, when we become adults and maybe leave his house one day, we will continue to follow and walk with God for the rest of our lives.

Therefore, we are happy with how Daddy is training us. We pray and study the Bible with him every day before we go to bed. We also pray for a few minutes after we come from school. Sometimes, we are tired, but it is a good habit to learn how to talk to God in prayer!

62. Why does God live forever but we, human beings, can't–or can we?

Did you ever want to live forever? Never get sick, or hungry, or tired? If you answered yes, you are not alone. I was particularly interested in knowing why God lives forever, but we cannot. Daddy then told us that God has no beginning and no end. But we, human beings, have a beginning. Although most human beings will die one day, all of them will live forever in another form after their death.

I used to think that human life begins at birth, but Daddy taught us that it begins when their mother is pregnant with them. People start living even before they are born. When each of us was a baby in our mother's womb, we were already living inside our mother's womb, but we were just not fully formed yet. It took about 9 months for a baby to develop and be ready to be born. Then, after babies are born, they start drinking milk or baby formula and growing until they become adults.

At this point, my brother Joshua-Enoch asked Daddy if women who have babies first drink milk, and then the baby drinks from the mom. *"That is so gross,"* answered my sister and I.

Daddy replied that no question is gross, and every question needs to be asked so an answer can be given and people can know better. No mother feeds her baby milk just because she first drank milk. When humans eat, food enters their belly and takes different forms before the body can take it and use it. The part of the food that the body doesn't take comes out of the body in the form of poop or pee. Part of the food that we eat goes to the blood. For some women who have a baby, part of the food goes to their breasts, where it is transformed into milk. When a mommy puts her breast in her baby's mouth, even if the baby is one day old, the baby starts squeezing the breast and takes the milk as food. Sometimes, when the babies are older and have teeth, they can hurt their mother if they bite their breasts. Some women who have babies are not able to produce milk in their breasts, and they have to buy baby formula and mix it with water so they can feed their babies. Otherwise, the babies will be very hungry and even die, which is not a good thing.

As Daddy said this, I asked him, *"How does the mommy give the baby milk when the baby is still inside of her?"*

Daddy replied that babies don't drink milk before they are born, but they eat and get everything they need from their mommy's blood through something called an umbilical cord, which connects the baby's belly to the mom's belly. After the baby is born, the umbilical cord is cut, and the mark later shows up as the belly button.

It may sound gross that babies eat blood, but that is how it goes. After babies are born, they don't eat or drink blood anymore, but they start eating liquid food like milk until their intestines are ready to digest harder food. In other words, if you give a baby adult food, they cannot digest it, but they will get sick and can even die. This is because everything on earth has its time. Carnivores, animals that eat meat, are the main ones that like drinking blood after they are born. That is why they kill other animals and eat their fresh meat and blood. Now that we answered how milk is formed, let's go back to our question about why God can live forever, but people cannot.

Indeed, after people are born, they can die anytime if death strikes them. However, death is not the end of human life. When people die, their spirit and soul continue to live in another form. Those who believe in God will live forever in heaven, while those who refuse to believe in God will live in hell forever. This means that all human beings have a beginning, but will live forever. But God is the only one who has been living before everything was created, and He will live forever.

63. Why is God bigger than the world, yet He created certain small things?

Daddy liked hearing us ask such a great question. As he answered, he said that if God wanted to create a world bigger than the current world, He could have done so. But He chose to create the world as it is.

Certain things are small, but others are big. Because God is the most powerful and greatest of all, He did not want to create a world or anything greater than Himself. God is above everything, and everything He created must obey Him and honor Him. Everything that wants to be greater than God will be brought down. We human beings worship God. Although we don't know how animals, plants, and even celestial bodies communicate with God, it is possible that they have their own ways of honoring God. Even the flowers in the field glorify God with their beauty, and they also make many people happy.

God created everything in the universe for a specific reason and mission. Even the smallest things have their places and missions. Not because certain things are very big does it mean that they are always more important than the smallest ones. For instance, babies are smaller than adults, yet babies are very important. Every adult was once a baby. If human beings were not born as babies but as adults, it would have been impossible for their mother to birth them. For, they will be too big to come out of the belly. Even if pregnant women birth babies as gigantic as adults, it will be hard for those adult babies to stay in a stroller, and they can break mommy's shoulder if she tries to pick them up.

Therefore, it is a good thing that people are born as babies and then grow. If the adults don't take care of their babies very well, God is not happy, and one day all adults can die, and nobody else will be on the planet to replace them. Hence, parents take care of their babies and buy them food to eat and good toys to play with, even if they play with them in the mud. This means that God creating things smaller than Him is ok. Although we see many small things in the world, galaxies are very huge, and the whole universe is very big. The universe is so big that scientists have not finished discovering it all yet. I don't think they will ever fully discover it. They have yet to discover many things on this Earth; hence, the universe that is much larger than the Earth has more things to discover than what is left undiscovered on Earth.

64. Why did God take six days to create everything?

We have learned in the Bible that God created the world in 6 days and rested on the 7th day. As we were compiling (meaning putting together) our questions to Daddy, Joelle-Major asked: *"Why did it take six days for God to create everything?"* Before answering this question, Daddy asked Joelle-Major why she asked that question. She answered that she thought that, because God is very powerful and can do anything, He could have taken just one day to create everything.

Daddy was happy at Joelle-Major because she knew that God is powerful and can do anything. Daddy was also super happy because he realized that his children were thinking very well and were trying to understand how Baby Universe was born. Daddy told us that, although God can do anything, He is very organized and likes to do things according to a specific plan and time. For example, a baby is not born in one day. It takes about 9 months for a baby to grow in the mother's womb before being born. In the same manner, when Mother Solar System was birthing the Sun and the planets, including the Earth, it took some time before each baby could move from where they were born, grow up, and become an adult celestial body.

By the time the Earth, the Moon, the Sun, and the other celestial bodies were formed, it took six days. But to be honest, Daddy said that, according to the math he did to calculate how the universe was born, some celestial bodies were fully formed after the first 6 days, but most of their babies were formed within the 6 days of creation. Everything God did was and is still for a reason. God created everything in 6 days to serve as an example of what will happen after creation. For instance, God rested on the 7th day of creation for a reason.

As soon as Daddy said this, I asked him, *"Why does God have to rest when He never gets tired?"*

"What a great question, Josephine," Daddy replied. It is not that God was really tired, for He is almighty, all-powerful, and has everything. He does not need to sleep or catch a nap to be better. God does not need any medicine to stay healthy, for He never gets sick and is always healthy. He does not get hungry and does not need to eat food to be full. So, when God rested on the 7th day, he was just giving us an example that we would follow for years to come. For God wants human beings to work for 6 days and rest on the 7th day.

The Bible also said that one day for God is 1000 days for human beings. The Bible also seems to say that the world will end about 6000 years after it was created. The Bible says that when Jesus Christ returns to Earth for His second coming, He will rule as a king for 1000 years. In other words, the 6 days of creation are an example of the 6000 years that must pass before Jesus returns to Earth to rule for 1000 years, a time of rest for believers.

In summary, according to the Bible, the Earth is just a few thousand years old, not millions of years old as some scientists have guessed. Daddy did some math and showed that the Earth is less than 6000 years old.

We'd better listen to what the Bible says! By the time we reached this level of our

Nathanael-Israel Israel: Author of "Science180 Accurate Scientific Proof of God"

writing, Daddy had answered all of our questions. Yet, to be sure, Daddy asked us again if we had any more questions about the creation of the universe. And we said no, for all our questions were answered. But don't get me wrong; there were many questions that we asked Daddy, and he answered them all, but he did not put all of them in this book. Therefore, that was the end of this book!

Remember, Daddy wrote many more books for adults that you can check out or ask your parents and friends to check out at www.Science180.com. Remember to also follow Daddy on his website www.Israel120.com, where you can get free resources.

Thank you for reading this book. For any questions, please contact my Daddy, Dr. Nathanael-Israel Israel.

Nathanael-Israel Israel: Author of "Science180 Accurate Scientific Proof of God"

SECTION 13: RESOURCES FOR YOUR PARENTS OR THE ADULTS
IN YOUR HOME–NEXT STEPS OF THE JOURNEY

177
Science180: Understand the Origin of the Universe and Life. Increase Your
Glory and Peace of Mind

Because Daddy has so many funny stories, I thought that he would have to do other books for us about life and chemicals, just like he did for adults. If you are interested in learning more about my other Daddy's books, please visit www.Science180.com. or go to www.Israel120.com to talk to him.

65. Get free resources on Science180.com

If you have finished reading this book and would like to learn more about my discoveries and how they can help you, you are at the right place. Indeed, I am really committed to helping you address any questions that you may still have about the origin, functioning, and fate of the universe, and how you can partner or collaborate with me for greater results.

To get free resources that will help you understand other aspects of the universe's formation not covered in this book, visit Science180.com and my personal website, Israel120.com. On those sites, I will be sharing guides and strategies to get the most out of my initiatives. I will also be sharing my favorite references, tips, next steps, readings, and other important things in the pipeline that will help you, regardless of your field of expertise, interests, or needs.

66. Subscribe to "Science180 Newsletter": The only accurate universe-origin, life-origin, and chemicals-origin newsletter in the whole world!

Be a part of decoding the universe's origin, life's origin, and chemicals' origin! Get origin-related news, information, discoveries, updates, announcements, reviews, articles, educational materials, and opportunities, from a holistic perspective not available anywhere else, so you can participate in and enjoy decoding the origin, current state, and fate of the universe and its content. You will also receive priceless tips about how Nathanael-Israel thinks, what his secrets and initiatives are, what he has accomplished, and what he recommends. Without any delay, sign up for the Science180 Newsletter today at Science180.com/newsletter. It is free!

67. Speaking engagement

In addition to writing groundbreaking books and engaging in other business endeavors, Nathanael-Israel Israel is a renowned speaker whom you can invite to speak at your organization.

Values that Dr. Nathanael-Israel Israel can add to your life include:
- Rare expertise and tips that will increase your abilities

- Usefulness that will advance your impact regardless of your field of expertise
- Understanding of the world that will sharpen your perspective
- Critical information that will positively change your life
- Experiences turned into insight that will motivate and guide you
- Irrefutable scientific proofs of the existence of God that will save you time and launch you into a zone of unlimited opportunities
- Unquestionable scientific proofs of how God created the universe
- Accurate demonstration of the historic formula that reconciled science and the Bible
- Enlightenment that will help people including Christians to start using their brain instead of just praying and expecting God to do everything for them

For speaking inquiries, including how you can get Dr. Nathanael-Israel Israel to speak to your organization or at an event, visit Science180.com/speaking for more details.

As the standout scientific authority who accurately decoded the universe, Nathanael-Israel Israel has been helping countless people across the globe to discover and understand the complex origin of the universe without leaving out the challenging questions that people of all ages have been struggling to answer for thousands of years! As the true go-to expert when it comes to the formation of the universe and of life, Nathanael-Israel believes that, regardless of age, background, culture, religion, or profession, everyone deserves to understand how the universe and life were formed and how they can leverage that knowledge to improve lives nonstop. Therefore, his groundbreaking discoveries of the formation of the universe, life, and chemicals have been broken down into books tailored to scientists (including physicists, chemists, biologists, mathematicians), laypeople or the general public, believers, and freethinkers; philosophers; children; etc., therefore maximizing the benefits to humanity. These historic, internationally acclaimed origin books include:

- "Turbulent Origin of the Universe"
- "Reconciling Science and Creation Accurately"
- "Turbulent Origin of Chemical Particles"
- "From Science to Bible's Conclusions"
- "Turbulent Origin of Life"
- "Origin of the Spiritual World"
- "How Baby Universe Was Born"
- "How God Created Baby Universe"
- "Science180 Accurate Scientific Proof of God"
- "Mathematical Proof of God's Existence at the Intersection of Science and Faith"

HOW GOD CREATED BABY UNIVERSE

When you hire Nathanael-Israel Israel to speak at your organization, you will:

- get specific in-depth knowledge, up-to-the-minute information, ideas, and insights about the universe's origin, life's origin, and chemicals-origin so that you expand your market, cut useless costs, stop wasting time on inadequate projects, and start focusing on the profitable solutions
- get relevant universe-origin stories that are specific to your field of expertise
- learn from a cooperative, flexible, and an easy to work with expert who will respond to your universe formation needs and position you to stay on top of your competitors
- interact with a renowned expert who will not just lecture you, but will help you sort out your origin-related questions using strategies to tap into deep secrets you ignore
- listen to an experienced expert who discovered outstanding secrets about the origin of all there is
- learn authentic information not from someone who just reads you a PowerPoint, but from the true go-to expert (when it comes to critical cosmological problems) who will share with you both his mistakes and successes that will help you get much closer to the better life you want to live
- revolutionize every origin-related domain with your accurate understanding of the universe's origin
- scientifically learn how the Earth was formed on the 3rd day of creation
- logically learn how the Sun and the Moon were formed on the 4th day of creation
- hear Dr. Nathanael-Israel Israel's personal selection and teaching of key topics that will help you break the code of the universe's formation and functioning; and strategically enlighten you; and guide you to navigate and filter the massive data collected on the universe and its content so you know how to answer the world's most challenging origin questions, remove any scientific and philosophical cataracts that may be blocking you, and help bring you many steps closer to your best life today and forever
- hear the greatest scientific and philosophic lessons of some top scientists, philosophers, thinkers, and public figures who have realized historic mistakes they made in life (concerning the origin of the universe, life, and chemicals), and that they corrected thanks to the discoveries of Nathanael-Israel Israel, who founded Science180, and who is acknowledged as the scientist that truly decrypted the universe-origin for the first time
- Get world key lessons successful people have learned in life, and how people can learn from their experiences to improve their lives instead of repeating their mistakes that many people still ignore at their own perils

180
Nathanael-Israel Israel: Author of "Science180 Accurate Scientific Proof of God"

To book Dr. Nathanael-Israel Israel for a speaking engagement, visit Science180.com/speaking.

68. How the adult in your home can make money by joining the affiliate program to sell Nathanael-Israel Israel's books

Greetings,

Do you want to make easy money by selling the #1 universe-origin, life-origin, and chemicals-origin books on your website, newsletter, and by mail? You can start making big money as you help sell Science180 Books, including this one, on your website and network. Indeed, by now you know that I operate a website called Science180.com, which specializes in helping people around the globe scientifically decode and understand the formation of the universe, life, and chemicals.

Your contacts, site, blog, forum, podcast, and newsletter may be admired among my target audience. Some of my products and services may be of interest to your audience. My books are the first in history to scientifically demonstrate the match between science and Biblical creation in a way that satisfies both believers and nonbelievers, a historic achievement and discovery that is revolutionizing our view of the origin of the universe, life, and chemicals for the benefit of humankind.

Imagine you have a website where you can talk to people about my books and services, and get a great percentage of every purchase they make on my site? Imagine you send a link to my books to your friends or network, and when any of your contacts buy a copy, you get a percentage of what they pay on my sites. Imagine you can email your friends to spread the good news about my books, and when anyone uses that link to buy them, I give you something. Well! This is what the affiliate program is about. Apply today or learn more about it at Science180.com/affiliate. Likewise, if you own a website, you can apply for Science180's affiliate program, and I will send you a specific affiliate link that you will place on your website and newsletter, and if people click on it to buy my books, they will be led to my page, and after they buy, I will pay you a certain amount, sharing the profit with you instead of just verbally saying thank you.

Would you be interested in reviewing some of my products and services to explore becoming an affiliate? We have a wonderful affiliate program, and commissions are paid quickly and accurately.

If you are satisfied with the quality of our products and services, I am convinced you will also be impressed by our affiliate program.

I look forward to hearing from you

Nathanael-Israel Israel, PhD

Science180: Understand the Origin of the Universe and Life. Increase Your Glory and Peace of Mind

69. Collaborate or partner with Nathanael-Israel Israel

If you have any lawful idea, initiative, or suggestion for a genuine partnership with Dr. Nathanael-Israel Israel or Science180, please visit Science180.com/partner to inform us.

70. How to be trained or mentored by or have a one-on-one consulting with Dr. Nathanael-Israel Israel

Hire Nathanael-Israel Israel to train you or your organization in the best ways to conduct yourself and to align your initiatives with the real understanding of the origin of the universe, of life, and of chemical particles in a way that you will not hear anywhere else. Nathanael-Israel Israel offers training through the "Science180 Academy" program. For training purposes, please visit Science180Academy.com.

71. Visit Nathanael-Israel Israel's personal website to get great resources for free that you won't find anywhere else

To stay in touch with Dr. Nathanael-Israel Israel, and to get updates directly from him, please visit his website, Israel120.com, and sign up for his popular newsletter at Israel120.com/newsletter for free.

72. Ask for review

If you are a book reviewer or a professional wanting to review this book or others written by Nathanael-Israel Israel, please contact us at Science180.com/AskForReview

73. Donate and support Nathanael-Israel Israel's efforts and initiatives

To help humankind accurately understand the real origin of the universe and its content, as I have done in the groundbreaking books I published after 12 years of sacrifice, I need your financial support. If you can, please consider donating to me by visiting Israel120.com/donate or Science180.com/donate.

Your donation will help me continue doing what I did to bring these books to life, which you enjoyed and know will help many people across the globe. No amount of money is too small or too big. Whatever you can give, please give.

74. Quantity discounts: Purchase Science180 books including this one in bulk at a special discount

To purchase Science180 books, including this one, in bulk at a special discount for sales promotion, corporate gifts, fund-raising, or educational purposes, or to create special editions to specifications, visit Science180.com/discount.

75. Buy a copy of Nathanael-Israel Israel's books for your friends, family, or someone

If this book has been a blessing to you, and we know it has, please consider getting another copy and giving it to a friend, a family member, or someone you think it may help or challenge. If you want to get many copies, we can even give you a discount; just contact us as we previously explained.

76. Recommend Nathanael-Israel Israel's books to your organization

Because I know this book has been a blessing to you, I ask that you recommend it, along with others I wrote, to your organization, class, workplace, church, school, network, or clubs. Recommending this book will help others tap into the blessings and opportunities my books offer.

77. Share Nathanael-Israel Israel's groundbreaking discovery with others

To improve more lives, please share the findings of Nathanael-Israel Israel's books with others, for many people out there still do not understand how the universe was formed, and sharing your experience of reading this book will help them. If you enjoy Nathanael-Israel Israel's books, please help other people find them by writing a book review on your blog or on online bookstores, or write it and share it with us. Likewise, share and mention this book on your social media platforms (e.g., Facebook, Twitter, YouTube, etc.).

78. Follow Nathanael-Israel Israel on social media

In our modern world, social media has become a major factor in how messages spread across the globe. To ensure more people hear about the good news revealed in my books, I need you to follow me and share my content on your social media and in your network. To know the full list of my social media accounts and follow me, please visit Science180.com/socialmedia.

79. Share your feedback, critics, testimony, experience, adventures, story, or comment about this book with me

How have Nathanael-Israel Israel's books and services at Science180 improved your life? I would love to hear from you.

To better understand how I can help you next and encourage others, I need to capture your testimony or criticisms. Please visit the feedback page, Science180.com/feedback, to tell me:

- how this book impacted you or will impact you
- what you like or dislike or disagree with
- what you think, wish, or dream that I need to work on next
- what you wish to see in this book, but that was absent
- what shocked you the most
- what got your heart pumping as you were reading this book
- what you found more insightful or thought-provoking
- what you want to do to be a part of my journey
- how my work changed your life or someone else's life

80. Message from the publisher of this book

Just like Nathanael-Israel Israel, you can publish your book(s) with us, too. To get started and see how we may help you, please visit Science180Publishing.com today.

81. Science180 Books that will Help You or Your Parents!

'Science180 Academy' Success Strategy:
SCIENCE180 BOOKS THAT WILL HELP YOU OR YOUR PARENTS!

I, Nathanael-Israel Israel, broke down my discovery about the formation of the universe into many books so that you, the readers, can pick the ones that correspond to your needs and interests without disappointing you or wasting your precious time. These books come in many versions (e.g., scientific version, public version, chemical version, biological version, biblical or prophetic version, pseudepigraphic version, and a children's version) targeting people according to their expertise, educational background, and interests as briefed below:

1. **"TURBULENT ORIGIN OF THE UNIVERSE"** (This is the scientific version of my book tailored to scientists and anyone interested in the detailed scientific demonstration of the universe formation). In this book I used the "mother of all turbulences" to scientifically demonstrate the formation of the universe so that scientists can understand and reorient the course of their research, teaching, and publishing and accept the truth to better live today and forever. Get *"Turbulent Origin of the Universe"* today to begin an incredible journey of accurately decoding the universe and change your life forever! Learn more at Science180.com/scientific

2. **"RECONCILING SCIENCE AND CREATION ACCURATELY"** (this is the book that I called the "Biblical or prophetic version of my book on the universe's origin, and it targets Christians and anyone interested in knowing the Biblical perspective of the creation of the universe). This important book accurately demonstrates the marvelous creation and formation of the universe by God in six consecutive 24-hour-days, and answers many questions about the universe's creation so that after acknowledging Him (who deserves all the glory now and forever), human beings can choose life and avoid the terrible judgment awaiting the unbelievers in the world to come. Get this thoughtful book now to figure out what happened at the beginning, what is coming up, and why it is time to urgently rethink everything you have been told about the universe's origin so you don't eventually regret! Don't say I did not tell you! Learn more at Science180.com/biblical

3. **"TURBULENT ORIGIN OF CHEMICAL PARTICLES"** (Called the "chemical version" of my book on the universe's origin, this elegant book targets chemists, biochemists, and anyone interested in chemistry). With *"Turbulent Origin of Chemical Particles"*, the accurate decrypting and understanding of the formation of chemicals has never been profitable and easy. Hence this great book is THE ultimate how-to guide for great people wanting to correctly decode the origin of the chemicals and positively transform their lives. Get this celebrated book today. Learn more at Science180.com/chemical

4. **"ORIGIN OF THE SPIRITUAL WORLD"** (This book is what I called the pseudepigraphic or hidden version of my books on the universe origin, and it is meant for believers who want to tap into a higher level of scriptural secrets that most people may not believe). This book draws the attention of the world toward the pseudepigrapha (a collection of hidden and rejected books, yet filled with deep secrets still valuable today) and explaining how, for thousands of years, God has already revealed deep details about the supernatural origin of the universe, but people (including those who believe or claim to believe in Him) have just refused to literally accept God's mysterious story of creation, which can never be understood by just sticking with conventional science. If you believe in God but have some origin-related questions whose answers you cannot find anywhere, not even in the Bible, and if you want to tap into historically neglected revelations to answer fundamental universe and life questions, then be sure to get a copy of *"Origin of the Spiritual World"* today. Learn more at Science180.com/pseudepigrapha

5. **"FROM SCIENCE TO BIBLE'S CONCLUSIONS"** (I called this book the "public version" of my book on the origin of the universe and it is tailored for the general public, and it is a great summary of the scientific version from a perspective that laypeople will fully understand). In this book, I, Nathanael-Israel Israel, broke down the complicated (scientific, philosophical including religious) data about the origin of the universe in a simple language that the general public can fully understand, and know in order to live happily forever. Quickly grab and read this scientifically verifiable, bestselling book to finally get the accurate, jaw-dropping answer that has been rationally shaking believers, skeptics, and all freethinkers. Don't wait! Learn more at Science180.com/public

6. *"TURBULENT ORIGIN OF LIFE"* (This is the biological or life version of my book on the origin of the universe). It is meant to suit scientists, nonscientists, and all kids of laypeople, and it decodes the origin of all forms of life so human beings can understand and better live. As of 2025, this book is my only book devoted to the origin of all forms of life, and it will help you to grasp in a simple language what is needed to fully understand the formation of all forms of life. Whether you are a scientist or a layperson, a believer, or a skeptic, you cannot afford to ignore the greater, better, faster, simpler, cheaper, easier, and accurate formula unlocked in this important book that successfully decoded the origin of life. Get *"Turbulence Origin of Life"* today and change lives. Don't wait. Learn more at Science180.com/life

7. *"HOW BABY UNIVERSE WAS BORN"* (How was the universe formed? Did God really form it like some people believe, or did it come out of some long processes? How can we scientifically prove and break down this difficult mystery in a language that children will fully understand and like?) Get the answers as you read this book that I called the "children version" of my book on the origin of the universe and life. Accurately explaining the complex formation of the universe and of life to children can be very hard in our modern world, but by getting *"How Baby Universe was Born"*, you will know the proven formula to help children to easily understand their huge universe-origin and life-origin questions with confidence, humor, and joy. They will surely belly laugh and thank you for it! It is time to buy this pragmatic book and offer it to the children in your life today. Learn more at Science180.com/children

8. **"HOW GOD CREATED BABY UNIVERSE"**. The most difficult part of writing scientific things to children is how to break down complex technical concepts into simple words that they and even anyone who can read and clearly understand (without losing the accurate details and facts). When the topic to address is about the origin of the universe, the task is even more challenging for most people, but not for Nathanael-Israel Israel. As long as you can read, you will find this amazing book extremely helpful to grasp all complicated concepts needed to properly crack the origin of the universe in a language that even children ages 7-12 and anyone who did not go very far in school can fully comprehend.

Science180: Understand the Origin of the Universe and Life. Increase Your Glory and Peace of Mind

9. *"SCIENCE180 ACCURATE SCIENTIFIC PROOF OF GOD"* (Whether you are a believer, an unbeliever, a freethinker, an administrator, a politician, a curriculum designer, a curriculum specialist, an education policymaker, a librarian, a school board member, a parent, a researcher, a student, a teacher, clergy, or a layperson, as long as you are really seeking to scientifically understand the rational proof of the existence of God, *"Science180 Accurate Scientific Proof of God"* is the much-admired book written for great people just like you). As long as you are interested in the first and the only scientific book that talks to anti-creationists, evolutionists, big bang proponents, atheists, and all other freethinkers and rationalists about the universe's formation and they bigly beg to know more about God, the creator, whom they mistakenly deny; then this book is for you. As long as you are really seeking to scientifically understand the rational proof of the existence of God, *"Science180 Accurate Scientific Proof of God"* is the much-admired book written for great people just like you. Grab it today and start reading it. Don't wait any longer! Learn more at Science180.com/godproof

If you want to have the entire big picture of my discovery of the origin of the universe, life, and chemicals, and to enlighten your life and career, then plan to get all or some of these books that best suit your needs and interests. For more details, visit Science180.com/books

Below are more details on each of these books.

Another Book by Nathanael-Israel Israel:
TURBULENT ORIGIN OF THE UNIVERSE

THE FIRST AND ONLY SCIENTIFIC BOOK THAT ACCURATELY EXPLAINS EVERYTHING YOU NEED TO UNCONVENTIONALLY, EASILY, AFFORDABLY, AND ENJOYABLY DECODE THE UNIVERSE FORMATION

In *"Turbulent Origin of the Universe"*, filled with great diagrams and digestible scientific facts, you will discover, learn, or get:

- The all-in-one, proven & uncomplicated scientific formula that accurately decoded the formation of the universe, and that explained the birthdate of the stars, planets, satellites, asteroids, and all other celestial bodies in the universe, so you can position yourself to stay on top of your competitors and avoid repeating crucial mistakes that many people have ignorantly made at their own perils

- Extraordinary, unprecedented, accurate insights into the first factors (e.g. early universe physics) that defined the history and formation of the universe so you can tap into deep scientific secrets you ignore, and set yourself apart from others

- The new physics that will revolutionize science forever and land you into a zone of original ideas that improve lives nonstop regardless of your expertise

- The 4 simple things without which it is impossible for anyone to ever understand the formation of the universe, think accurately, work differently, achieve, or perform better for superior results

- The verified key to move the cosmological mountains of misunderstanding, so you can confidently free your mind from doubts, improve your health, and prevent you from any danger connected with sticking with wrong assumptions

- Save time and money, and enjoy your life once you remove errors holding your true understanding of the universe's origin captive

- Historic scientific proof of whether a planet was formed in 2.82 days, whether a satellite was formed in 3.32 days, and whether a star was formed in 3.69 days after the beginning of the universe; so you can creatively produce and address a broader work spectrum by learning how to effectively communicate with and establish unusual connections between otherwise disconnected and disparate scientific data

- The scientific formula that successfully tested the existence of God in a way that shocked believers, skeptics, and all other freethinkers
- Why the scientific community has failed to sufficiently explain the origin of the universe and understand how existing theories have missed and undefined central ideas, and imposed limits on the vision of scientists
- Specific in-depth knowledge, up-to-the-minute information, and ideas so you can expand your market, cut useless costs, stop wasting time on inadequate projects, and start focusing on the profitable solutions (Science180.com/scientific)
- How Science180 Academy can strategically enlighten you and guide you to navigate and filter the massive data collected on the universe, so you can answer the world's most challenging questions, remove any scientific and philosophical cataracts that may be blocking you, and bring you many steps closer to your best life
- How to better resonate with your target market that is craving something original that breaks wrong explanations of the universe's origin

Get *"Turbulent Origin of the Universe"* today to begin an incredible journey of accurately decoding the universe and change your life forever!

Dr. Nathanael-Israel Israel is told by people that he is the #1 Universe-origin, Life-origin, and Chemicals-origin expert. He is the founder of Science180 and the author of many books on the origin of the universe and its content. To learn more about how he may help you, visit Israel120.com.

Another Book by Nathanael-Israel Israel:
RECONCILING SCIENCE AND CREATION ACCURATELY

THERE IS ONLY ONE SIMPLE, COMPELLING, SOLUTION-DIRECTED SCIENTIFIC FORMULA ACCURATE ENOUGH TO RATIONALLY EXPLAIN HOW GOD CREATED THE UNIVERSE

"Reconciling Science and Creation Accurately" is a landmark book in universe-origin writing from a rare perspective by one of the most respected minds of our time. It scientifically explores the most challenging questions of all times that believers, nonbelievers, and all freethinkers are interested in: How can we rationally demonstrate, without checking our brain at the door in the name of faith, that God created the universe? How did the universe begin and what processes did God use to create it? Are these processes still operating in the universe or not? Can believers abandon wrong theories if they think it is impossible for science to literally prove the Genesis story, or if they think that science is evil and diametrically opposed to faith, or if they compromisingly embrace scientific theories that contradict the Biblical account of creation written before the scientific era? What can believers do to help the skeptics believe in the Biblical narrative of creation?

Lucky you, Dr. Nathanael-Israel Israel successfully navigated all those questions with an accuracy that both scientists and nonscientists have been applauding across the globe. After reading *"Reconciling Science and Creation Accurately"*, you will confidently:

- Scientifically prove the Biblical account of the creation of the universe and the existence of God in a way that makes the head of those who deny God to spin faster than a DJ's turntable
- Know how to rationally talk to anti-creationists, evolutionists, Big Bang proponents, atheists, skeptics, and other freethinkers about the universe's formation and they will beg you to know more about God, the Creator, that they mistakenly rejected
- Discover very accurate, rare, and factual truths about the universe's origin that will save you time and money, and get you much closer to the better and joyful life you want to live today and forever
- Improve your health and faith by knowing that the existence of God can be scientifically justified using Science180 Cosmology and particularly Science180 Creationism
- Enter a new area of freedom and power by crushing the head of and breaking free from the suffocating expectations of all wrong theories that have hijacked secular and religious education, and that have held the Biblical account of creation captive for almost 3500 years

Science180: Understand the Origin of the Universe and Life. Increase Your Glory and Peace of Mind

- Break free from the suffocating expectations of some forms of creationism that have sequestered the mind of some believers for a long time
- Uncompromisingly, intelligently, and scientifically explode the myth of those who, instead of literally taking the Biblical days of creation as 24-hour consecutive days, think that they were millions of years, or were representative of long ages, or that millions of years existed before them or were positioned between them
- Understand the accurate standard to interpret the Biblical account of creation thanks to Science180's breakthrough that transformed science and laid a foundational bedrock for the inerrancy of Scripture

Now that Genesis (the oldest manuscript in the world, written before science and most religions were born) is scientifically proven to be correct (Science180.com/biblical), what unstoppable, jaw-dropping paradigm shift will the discovery of the perfect alignment between science and the Bible bring into the religious, rational, and secular world today? Get this thoughtful book now to figure out what happened at the beginning, what is coming up, and why it is time to urgently rethink everything you have been told about the universe's origin so you don't eventually regret! Don't say nobody told you!

Founder of Science180 Academy, **Dr. Nathanael-Israel Israel** is acknowledged worldwide as the discoverer of the all-in-one, proven, and simple scientific formula that accurately cracked the origin of the universe, of life, and of chemicals and that scientifically unearthed the holy grail at the intersection of science and the Biblical account of creation. Learn more at Israel120.com.

Another Book by Nathanael-Israel Israel:
TURBULENT ORIGIN OF CHEMICAL PARTICLES

FIND ALL THE RELIABLE, CONVINCING, SCIENTIFIC ANSWERS YOU NEED TO SUCCESSFULLY DECODE THE ORIGIN OF CHEMICAL PARTICLES SAFELY

Where did all elementary particles and composite particles including atoms, molecules, minerals, and rocks, come from? What are the fundamental factors, the machinery, and the generic processes that defined their formation and properties? What was the nature of their precursors at the beginning of the universe and what underlying processes shaped or molded them into the chemicals we know today? What was the primary cause of the abundance and diversity of chemicals in the celestial bodies in the universe? What is the accurate link between the formation of chemical particles and the formation of galaxies, stars, planets, asteroids, and satellites? What light can the origin of chemicals shed on the real cause and meaning of gravity and the other so-called fundamental forces in nature? How does the formation of the chemical particles fit into the big picture of the formation of the universe?

After studying these questions for more than 12 years, Dr. Nathanael-Israel Israel discovered that the proper understanding of the origin of chemical particles is a very challenging but profitable task that requires original, scientific, mathematical, and philosophic efforts beyond the current state of modern science—until recently. The solution for all of these puzzling problems: *"Turbulent Origin of Chemical Particles"*, the straightforward and trustworthy book that will help you to quickly, cheaply, easily, and efficiently navigate everything you need to know to finally solve the hard problems about the origin, the formation, and the functioning of all chemical particles. Whether you are a chemist, a biochemist, any other scientist, or an engineer, as long as you have a reasonable background in chemistry but ignore how to scientifically demonstrate the origin of all chemical particles, this marvelous book is for you!

Amazingly packed with eye-popping analysis, fantastic graphs, tables, and the historic formula that broke the universe-origin code, *"Turbulent Origin of Chemical Particles"* will:

- Make it easier than ever for you to properly understand, decrypt, and articulate the real origin of natural chemical particles in the universe, therefore freeing you from false and boring explanations of the origin of all matters, and embrace the proven theory that opens doors to unparallel opportunities

- Professionally teach you how to transform the true knowledge of the origin of chemical particles into insights that significantly add value to your life in less time, and successfully establish you as a symbol of freedom, power, creativity, and originality in your field of expertise

- Fire you up to become the best version of you, and to cause positive changes to your initiatives that will profit you nonstop
- Discover thrilling illustrations and unconventional explanations of the formation of all matter in the universe, written in a simple language that brings humankind much closer to the complete deciphering of the mysteries at the very heart of chemistry, and open the way to a future of technology, innovation, discoveries, and breakthroughs
- Equip you to bypass technical knowledge that restricts non-experts from accessing the origin-related secrets contained in the massive scientific data, and get to the bottom of origin-related mysteries regardless of your background so you can empower yourself to leave unforgettable marks in your field of expertise
- Learn more at Science180.com/chemical

With *"Turbulent Origin of Chemical Particles,"* the accurate decrypting and understanding of the formation of chemicals has never been profitable and easy. Hence this great book is THE ultimate how-to guide for great people wanting to correctly decode the origin of the chemicals and positively transform their lives. Get this celebrated book today. Don't wait!

Known as the nonconformist, rule-breaker, and accurate demonstrator of the universe's origin, **Dr. Nathanael-Israel Israel** is the founder of Science180, the one-stop for answering the most crucial universe and life's origin questions. He has had the honor to be acknowledged as the fearless universe-origin decryption trailblazer. Learn more at Israel120.com.

Another Book by Nathanael-Israel Israel:
ORIGIN OF THE SPIRITUAL WORLD

ONLY ONE ANCIENT BLUEPRINT HAS THE RELIABLE POWER TO HELP YOU TO ACCURATELY DECRYPT THE SPIRITUAL ORIGIN AND HISTORY OF EVERYTHING IN THE UNIVERSE

Countless books talk about the origin of the universe and of life, but this amazing book is the first and the only one that has undeniably explained how the formation of the universe and everything in it was truly revealed in the rejected and hidden scriptures such as the Books of Enoch and others. In *"Origin of the Spiritual World,"* you will:

- Discover deep-rejected secrets that have prevented humankind from unearthing the beginning of the universe
- Plainly see the scientific proof (hidden in scriptures) of the formation of the Earth, the Moon, and the Sun in a matter of days, a historic revelation that bizarrely and shockingly matches the scientific data as scientifically proved in *"From Science to Bible's Conclusions"*, a popular book written by Dr. Nathanael-Israel Israel
- Properly use the lost and rejected scriptures to articulate the process by which the universe was formed, and use that insight to improve your understanding of the Bible, innovate in your domain of interest, and improve your life perpetually
- Empower and align yourself with the historic breakthrough that has done what no other discovery has ever done: accurately unlock and decode mysteries concerning the origin of the cosmos and its content using scientific keys revealed in ancient scriptures that some elites have concealed (Science180.com/pseudepigraphic)
- Discover and apprehend the complex formation of the universe and life without leaving out the challenging questions that people of all ages have been struggling to answer for thousands of years, while the answers were hidden
- Find more joy in life through a clear interpretation of old and fresh revelations about the creation of the universe astonishingly backed by modern science, which some people wrongly think opposes the Bible
- Make a difference and blaze new trails for those who depend on your leadership

If you believe in God, have some origin-related questions whose answers you cannot find anywhere, not even in the Bible, and if you want to tap into historically neglected revelations to answer fundamental universe and life questions, then be sure to get a copy of *"Origin of the Spiritual World"* today.

Dr. Nathanael-Israel Israel happens to be the discoverer of the historic mathematical equations that scientifically demonstrated that the Earth was formed 2.82 days, the Moon 3.32 days, and the Sun 3.69 days after the beginning of the universe, therefore confirming the Biblical account of creation that revealed about 3500 years ago that the formation of the Earth was completed on the 3rd day, while that of the Moon and the Sun was completed on the 4th day of creation. Nathanael-Israel Israel is referred to as the "Undisputable Specialist of all Questions at the Intersection of Science and Biblical Creation". Learn more about this rare scientist at Israel120.com.

Nathanael-Israel Israel: Author of "Science180 Accurate Scientific Proof of God"

Another Book by Nathanael-Israel Israel:
FROM SCIENCE TO BIBLE'S CONCLUSIONS

THE # 1 UNIVERSE-ORIGIN MASTERPIECE OF ALL TIME … AND THE MOST ACCURATE SCIENTIFIC FORMULA THAT STOOD AND WILL STAND THE TEST OF TIME AND OF MATHEMATICS

The real reason scientists have been struggling to accurately understand the universe-formation is because they have spent centuries collecting expensive, complicated, and massive amounts of data, but learned very little, if not nothing, about how to unconventionally step back to properly analyze it to decode the universe. Consequently, people learned to collect all kinds of data everywhere to build models and imaginary concepts that betray their discernment, but they never learned to unlearn wrong theories, nor learned how to stop trashing great raw data hidden in theories they dislike or misunderstand; they never knew where to find and how to properly combine the fundamental variables without which it is impossible to ever clear the way so their data can properly work for and precisely lead them to the real origin of the universe. How can people abandon the dangerous theories they think are correct because they don't know any better ones?

Lucky you, that is where Dr. Nathanael-Israel Israel, the founder of Science180 (Science180.com) came in to properly reanalyze and put under control these costly, underrated data to provide the accurate and simple solution people have been looking for throughout the ages, but that they have ignored.

In *"From Science to Bible's Conclusions"*, you will:

- Get a world class explanation of the 4 fundamental variables without which it is unquestionably impossible to ever decode the universe-formation scientifically

- Save time and money, and enjoy a life filled with the wonderful peace that the accurate understanding of the universe's origin can create

- Discover the errors in the scientific theories and religious belief systems about the universe-formation that are putting you at risk, and learn how to take control over cosmological threats lurking at the edge of your rational mind, faith, disbelief, or doubt

- Unlock the accurate scientific formula to rationally test the existence of God in a historic way that uncompromisingly satisfies both believers and skeptics (Science180.com/public)

- Get all you need to become a knowledgeable person who will never again need anybody else to explain to you the origin of the universe, for, you will fully understand and articulate it yourself and rationally know whether science is really at war with religion

Science180: Understand the Origin of the Universe and Life. Increase Your Glory and Peace of Mind

- Receive deep insights that even those who went to university for years were not able to decrypt by themselves, so you can equip yourself to eliminate all forms of scientific and religious universe-origin prejudices
- Discover whether the scientific data finally confirms that the formation of the Earth was completed on the 3rd day, while that of the Moon and the Sun was on the 4th day of creation like the Bible says, or whether the data proves that it took billions of years to progressively form the universe
- Understand the celebrated scientific formula that rationally puts to rest all debates about the relationship between science, faith, and all theories about the universe's origin so you can properly develop yourself, expand your network, and shape your future

Quickly grab and read this scientifically verifiable, bestselling book to finally get the accurate, jaw-dropping answer that has been rationally shaking believers, skeptics, and all freethinkers. Don't wait!

Dr. Nathanael-Israel Israel has had the honor to be acknowledged as the #1 universe-origin, life-origin, and chemicals-origin expert. He is the author of *"Turbulent Origin of the Universe"*, *"Reconciling Science and Creation Accurately"*, *"Turbulent Origin of Chemical Particles"*, *"Turbulent Origin of Life"*, *"How Baby Universe Was Born"*, *"Science180 Accurate Scientific Proof of God"*. Visit Israel120.com to learn more about this world's most trusted expert that helps scientists and laypeople to properly decode the origin and formation of the universe, life, and chemicals so people can live more effectively nonstop.

Another Book by Nathanael-Israel Israel:
TURBULENT ORIGIN OF LIFE

THE ONLY ACCURATE FORMULA TO SCIENTIFICALLY EXPLAIN THE FORMATION OF ALL FORMS OF LIFE QUICKLY

Every human being will benefit from understanding the real origin of life. But the problem is that most efforts to explain the origin of life are complex, inaccurate, confusing, partisan, and complicated, therefore, creating serious challenges to those who are eager to scientifically decrypt where all forms of life came from. Most people want an accurate, simple, straightforward, nonpartisan life-origin book that is free from jargon and difficult concepts only known by the experts. This elegant scientific book breaks down the technicality of the origin of life in a language that even the nonscientists can easily comprehend. It is a trustworthy book that will help you to quickly, cheaply, easily, and efficiently navigate everything you need to know to finally decode and solve the puzzling problems about the origin of life, while also giving you a crash course on the universe's origin.

Unlike any book you have ever read on the origin of life, this historic masterpiece (that distills complex scientific data down to simple explanations that make sense) is the starting point of any smart person wanting to rationally understand the formation of all living things. By the time you finish reading "*Turbulent Origin of Life*", you will discover:

- Why in spite of the massive amount of scientific data collected on living things, scientists have misunderstood the formation of life until now, and then uncover in a simple language the one thing that was needed to accurately crack the code of life but that scientists have missed and that has been causing them headaches, overwhelm, and burnout

- Step-by-step pathway to decode the origin of life and get the power, freedom, and boldness to take advantage of the opportunities that accurate understanding of the origin of life creates (Science180.com/life)

- The high connection between the code of the universe formation and the process by which life on Earth was formed so you can become a fulfilled thought leader in your field of expertise

- Tools to stand as a lighting bolt that electrifies those who are still struggling to understand the formation of all forms of life in the universe

- Strategies to push the boundaries of human abilities to properly understand what is perceived as un-understandable, mysterious, supernatural, unimaginable, impossible, and unthinkable that hold people back

- Scientific approach to holistically detect, correct, and remove all misinformation, ambiguity, and misleading claims and theories surrounding the origin of life

Whether you are a scientist or a layperson, a believer or a skeptic, you cannot afford to ignore the greater, better, faster, simpler, cheaper, easier, and accurate formula unlocked in this important book that successfully decoded the origin of life. Get *"Turbulence Origin of Life"* today and change lives! Don't wait!

Dr. Nathanael-Israel Israel is the Father of Science180 Cosmology and the Founder of Science180 Academy. He is fortunate to be known as the source of unconventional wisdom and knowledge that help people accurately crack the code of the formation of the universe, of life, and of chemicals. Get some resources by visiting his personal website at Israel120.com.

Another Book by Nathanael-Israel Israel:
SCIENCE180 ACCURATE SCIENTIFIC PROOF OF GOD

THE FIRST AND THE ONLY SCIENTIFIC BOOK THAT TALKS TO ANTI-CREATIONISTS, EVOLUTIONISTS, BIG BANG PROPONENTS, ATHEISTS, AND ALL OTHER FREETHINKERS AND RATIONALISTS ABOUT THE UNIVERSE'S FORMATION, AND THEY BEG TO KNOW MORE ABOUT GOD, THE CREATOR, WHOM THEY DENY.

As you read this historic book, you will:

- Scientifically know what is the one clear sign you should always pay attention to in your efforts to decipher the primary cause and the key drivers of the fundamental processes responsible for universe formation.
- Discover the only way to scientifically know if God exists and, if so, which of the thousands of beings worshipped across the globe is the true God
- Accurately answer the most critical universe-origin and life-origin questions so you can stop standing in tension with consequential question marks, including those related to religion and reason or the so-called war between science and the Bible
- Discover the errors in the scientific and religious theories about the universe-origin and life-origin that are putting you at a high risk you will never recover from if you don't quickly and confidently learn how to rationally take control over threats lurking at the edge of your efforts to understand the universe and life today
- Challenge the cosmological status quo and embrace the real change that will disrupt the hidden cages that may be holding you and that you ignore
- Definitively answer all your doubts about the source or author of the universe and life ... (learn more at Science180.com/godproof)
- Understand that religion or faith, reason or science can coexist and can be properly reconciled to accurately lead you to the correct source of everything in the universe
- Satisfy your burning desire for freedom from beliefs and scientific theories about the universe's origin and life-origin that suffocate you and bind your mind, faith, unbelief, heart, and education
- Scientifically set on fire all false theories or dogmas about the existence of God, the Creator, that are enslaving humankind

Science180: Understand the Origin of the Universe and Life. Increase Your Glory and Peace of Mind

Whether you are a believer, unbeliever, freethinker, administrator, politician, curriculum designer, curriculum specialist, education policymaker, teacher, librarian, school board member, researcher, parent, student, clergy, or a layperson, as long as you are really seeking to scientifically understand the rational proof of the existence of God, *"Science180 Accurate Scientific Proof of God"* is the much-admired book written for great people just like you! Grab your copy today and start reading it! Don't wait any longer!

Dr. Nathanael-Israel Israel is a Beninese-American scientist, entrepreneur, and international consultant, who shows people of all ages and educational backgrounds how to scientifically decode the formation of the universe and of life, and who is acknowledged as the creator of the Chemicals Turbulent Origin Formula™, the inventor of the Life Turbulent Origin Formula™, and the discoverer of the Universe Creation Formula™. He is the Founder of Science180 Academy, which is trailblazing the reconciliation between science and the creation.

Nathanael-Israel Israel: Author of "Science180 Accurate Scientific Proof of God"

82. 'Science180 Academy' Success Strategy for your Parents or the Adults in your Home

Because this book is written for children and their parents, below are some materials that your parents or the adults in your house may enjoy. If you don't understand all of these materials, don't worry.

Science180: Understand the Origin of the Universe and Life. Increase Your Glory and Peace of Mind

'Science180 Academy' Success Strategy:
SCIENCE180 INTERVIEW REPORT (AKA SCIENCE180 INTERNET-TV-RADIO INTERVIEW REPORT)

Science180 Interview Report is the newsletter to read for guests and unconventional show ideas at the intersection of science and faith. Indeed, many hot questions are still unanswered on the road leading to the correct understanding of the origin of the universe, of life, and of chemicals. But most people don't know where to find the accurate answers to those challenging questions. What if with one simple call you can accurately answer all of those questions. You need to get in touch with or interview Dr. Nathanael-Israel Israel on your show, radio, tv, podcast, and even website, or invite him for a live presentation at your organization if your audience can benefit from any of the following show, talk, speaking, or interview ideas:

- Can we explain the formation of the universe through natural processes without evoking evolution and Big Bang?
- Are you convinced that it is a waste of time to attempt to prove the Bible is true by means of science or historical investigation?
- Is it a waste of time to attempt to prove the Biblical creation using science or historical investigation?
- How to scientifically prove that God created the universe without talking about the Bible
- How can we fix the tremendously dangerous trend according to which more people are denying God at the profit of secular theories because they think that it is impossible for science and faith to meet?
- How does the Biblical account of creation help to defend the accuracy of the Bible and the existence of God?
- How to talk to evolutionists, Big Bang proponents, atheists, and all other freethinkers about the universe formation and they will beg you to teach them more about God, the Creator?
- What needs to be done about the dangerous trend according to which many Christians are abandoning their faith at the profit of secular doctrines that deny creation because they have been disappointed in and victimized by their creationist theories?
- What needs to be done to fix the extremely dangerous trend that causes more and more people to embrace evolutionism and trash the Biblical account of creation as if the Bible lied about the 6 days of creation?
- Why are most nations (governments) wasting millions of dollars on universe-origin and life-origin research they don't need–or do they?

Nathanael-Israel Israel: Author of "Science180 Accurate Scientific Proof of God"

- Can you really be scientifically 100% sure and prove that God created the universe?
- Can atheists, rationalists, and all other freethinkers talk themselves out of denying God?
- Can Christians talk themselves out of doubting God and the Biblical account of creation?
- Is accurately understanding the universe's origin a choice?
- Why is it so challenging for people today to choose the right explanation of the universe's origin?
- Is accurately understanding the origin of chemical particles a choice?
- Why are Christians abandoning wrong creationist theories that compromise with Darwinism and Big Bang?
- What are the 4 surprising essential skills for smart people to crack the universe's origin?
- How to raise rational children in our modern world?
- What was it like to discover the "Scientific Formula of the Universe's Origin"?
- What is the one simple scientific formula that will make anyone pay attention to the Bible?
- How people, including some fervent Christians, come to believe lies about creation and what they can do to change them so atheists can enjoy God.
- Why do secular rationalists and freethinkers think that Christians are irrational?
- What are the 3 world-shaking truths about the separation of science and faith nobody ever told you?
- Is faith better than science?
- Why freethinkers and rationalists enjoyed rejecting the most rational story told before the birth of science and how it affects their search for the truth
- Why arguments against secular science are NOT arguments for creation
- What is the only scientific story that atheists and evolutionists hear and automatically believe in the existence of God? Period.
- Can we explain the formation of the universe through natural processes without invoking evolution and Big Bang?

I know you may be tempted to answer these questions by yourselves, but avoid landing yourself on wrong paths that caused some people to lose contact with reality, it is better to get the accurate answer from the know-how expert, Dr. Nathanael-Israel Israel, the author of many books on the origin of the universe, of life, and of chemicals, and the standout expert who accurately decoded the scientific formula that forces science to bow to the Bible. If you would like to register for Science180 Interview Report so we can periodically send you show ideas and opportunities related to the origin of the universe, of life, and of chemical particles, please visit Science180Interviews.com for more details. Nathanael-Israel Israel can also help you answer all of these questions accurately.

'Science180 Academy' Success Strategy:
SCIENCE180 ACADEMY

Science180 Academy is a training, speaking, consulting, and mentoring program designed to groom and empower people of all backgrounds in the truth about the origin of the universe, life, and chemicals. According to their background and interest, trainees are taught different levels of scientific facts to grasp a deeper understanding of the origin of the universe, how to properly think to unearth mysteries hidden in the massive scientific data collected across the globe but which is unfortunately less analyzed. If you want to be enlightened and equipped so you can cause positive changes in your respective field of expertise, then Science180 Academy program is for you.

Science180 Academy does not confer college credit, grant degrees, or grade its attendants, participants, or students. It is not an accredited university or college, but is the one-stop-destination for universe-origin, life-origin, and chemicals-origin experts. It is where scientists and laypeople get all their origin-related questions properly answered. It is the only place where the accurate interpretation of the universe-origin, life-origin, and chemicals-origin data matters a lot.

Science180 Academy brings together Dr. Nathanael-Israel Israel (the Founder of Science180) and other experts to deliver outstanding value, insight, and lessons to assist you to accurately understand the true origin of the universe, chemicals, and life, so you can tap into that knowledge to improve lives perpetually. Nathanael-Israel's goal is to give you practicable and undeniable proofs of the formation of the universe so you can be fired up to become the best version of you, and to cause positive changes to your initiatives that will profit you today and forever. For Nathanael-Israel, decoding the origin of the universe and everything in it is not a job, but his life mission, and helping others to fully understand that is his mission. Visit Science180Academy.com today to start.

If you are still wondering if Science180 Academy is for you, let me also inform you that some of Science180's clients and prospects have a profound technical knowledge and background in science, while others don't. Some are creationists (e.g. Science180 creationism, Young Earth creationists, Old Earth creationists, and Intelligent Design proponents); others are anti-creationists. Some are believers, others are freethinkers (including atheists, humanists, rationalists, agnostics, nontheists, nonreligious people, skeptics, nonbelievers, the religiously unaffiliated, spiritual-not-religious, ex-believers, and doubters). Regardless of their background, belief, or disbelief, Science180 works with each of these people to figure out their needs, priorities, and the products and services that best fit them.

Science180 improves their knowledge, experience, performance, and answer their questions (related to the universe-origin, life-origin, and chemicals-origin) by crafting a personalized program that perfectly matches their interests, needs, and things that are dear and meaningful to them whether it is to:

- Scientifically test and know whether there is a God that created the universe or not, and which God it is
- Become the leader that captures the heart of people craving for an unconventional explanation of the creation of the universe, life, and chemicals
- Free yourself from boring explanations of the origin of the universe, life, and chemicals and embrace the proven theory that opens doors to unparallel opportunities
- Disrupt all scientific chains of repetitive nonsenses about the universe-origin, life-origin, and turn your attention toward unconventional ideas leading to greater innovation and prosperity
- Satisfy your burning desire for freedom from beliefs and scientific theories about the universe's origin and life-origin that suffocate you and bind your mind, faith, unbelief, heart, and education
- Empower yourself to leave unforgettable marks and to stand tall as a symbol of freedom, power, creativity, and originality in your field of expertise
- Learn to set on fire all false universe-origin theories and life-origin theories that are enslaving humankind
- Fearlessly push the boundaries of the human abilities to properly understand what is perceived as un-understandable, mysterious, supernatural, unimaginable, impossible, and unthinkable that holds you back
- Participate in the global effort that is lighting an unquenchable fire under all nonsenses about the origin of the cosmos

To register or to learn more, visit Science180Academy.com today.

Science180 Academy deals with different subjects according to the needs of its members or target groups. When people register for Science180 Academy, they must choose the program(s) they want to focus on so their training can be properly personalized accordingly. This is similar to how people register for a university, and take classes in a specific department matching their needs!

Science180's breakthroughs are so complex and dense that it is not realistic or good to try to explain all in just one academy, else people will be overwhelmed, disinterested, and confused by the plethora of data to handle. In other words, Science180 Academy offers a wide range of origin-related training in various domains strategically designed to allow people to choose the most suitable for their needs so that, regardless of their background or field of expertise, people can equip themselves, align their mindset, and improve lives today and forever using the accurate explanation of the origin of the universe, of life, and of chemicals. Science180 Academy curriculum is based on 12 years of deep unconventional research that culminated with the publication of many much-admired books on the formation of the universe and its content:

The content of each Science180 Academy is strategically crafted by Dr. Nathanael-Israel Israel (who is acknowledged as the world's internationally acclaimed authority in origin-related issues) to suit both scientists and nonscientists, religious and nonreligious people, and leaders as well as followers so they can fully decode the proofs of the formation of the universe, of life, and of chemicals they have been wanting to demonstrate or grasp.

The current programs of Science180 Academy are:

- 1. **SCIENCE180 ACADEMY OF COSMOLOGY** (Designed for all scientists who want to scientifically study cosmology, the science of the origin and fate of the universe)

- 2. **SCIENCE180 ACADEMY OF TURBULENCE** (This is a perfect fit for scientists and other experts interested in studying abiotic turbulence).

- 3. **SCIENCE180 ACADEMY OF LIFE SCIENCES** (Tailored to those who want to study biotic turbulence)

- 4. **SCIENCE180 ACADEMY OF CHEMISTRY** (Designed for chemists, biochemists, scientists, and other educated people who want to understand the origin of chemical particles)

- **5. <u>SCIENCE180 ACADEMY FOR LAYPEOPLE OR THE GENERAL PUBLIC</u>** (Very fit for any layperson or "less" educated people who wants to learn (in a simple language) deep insights that even those who went to university for years were unable to decrypt by themselves, so these laypeople can be equipped to eliminate all forms of scientific and religious universe-origin prejudices.)

- **6<u>. SCIENCE180 ACADEMY FOR CHILDREN</u>** (This Academy breaks down origin key topics into language that children can fully understand). This is the only Science180 Academy that your whole family will like and enjoy together, and it will set children on the path of success by accurately showing them early in life the formation of the universe, and how to detect errors in theories or stories that would misguide them as they grow up. Therefore, you need to add this great, efficient, trustworthy, and cost-effective "Science180 Academy for Children" to the strategic journey of children toward their best tomorrow.

- **7. <u>SCIENCE180 ACADEMY OF THE PSEUDEPIGRAPHA AND SPIRITUAL WORLD</u>** (Only one ancient blueprint has the reliable power to help you to accurately decrypt the spiritual origin and history of everything in the universe. If you are a believer and want to delve into the prophetic, angelic, and higher order of knowledge based on the spiritual world, then this Science180 Academy is for you. This program is suitable for those who took at least "Science180 Academy of Creationism". For you to enjoy the courses in this Academy, you need to have at least learned about or attended Science180 Academy of Creationism. If not, you may waste your time trying to grasp simple and supernatural things that cannot be scientifically proven in this Academy, but in Science180 Academy of Creationism).

8. <u>SCIENCE180 ACADEMY OF CREATIONISM</u> (Science180 Creationism is a scientific theory spearheaded by the groundbreaking discoveries of Nathanael-Israel Israel, that scientifically explained the origin of the universe, life, and chemicals using turbulence and that mathematically reconciled science and the Biblical account of creation for the first time in history.

Science180 is different from all existing creationist theories known before 2025. Science180 Creationism reconciled science with the Biblical account of creation, including scientifically proving that the Earth was formed on Day 3, while the Moon and the Sun were formed on Day 4 of creation!). As you attend "Science180 Academy of Creationism", you will receive accurate answers to all your questions concerning the creation of the universe. The target audience of "Science180 Academy of Creationism" includes

- o Christians of all ages and all educational backgrounds
- o Christian or Bible colleges, universities, and schools
- o School boards of education and textbook initiative leaders
- o Churches, Christian ministries, televangelists, pastors, prophets, teachers, apostles, and all other ministers of God
- o Christian organizations
- o Anti-creationists wanting to explore the Biblical creation narrative

- **9. <u>SCIENCE180 ACADEMY FOR FREETHINKERS & ALL ANTI-CREATIONISTS</u>** (This Science180 Academy is designed for evolutionists, anti-creationists, and all other types of unbelievers seeking to rationally explore and understand alternative arguments for creation or formation or origin of the universe, life, and chemicals from a fresh, scientific perspective).

- o **10. <u>SCIENCE180 ACADEMY OF LEADERSHIP</u>**-(Also called "Science180 Academy for Leaders", this program will enlighten leaders of organizations on how to solve their people problems, process problems, and profit problems related to the origin of the universe, of life, and chemicals according to their domain of expertise). With "Science180 Academy of Leadership", leaders will gain new insights so they can cast new visions and avoid focusing on screwed-up processes, products, and services related to universe-origin initiatives that need to be fixed, faced, or dealt with. Science180 Academy of Leadership will also equip leaders to address process problems related to inefficiency, gaps, missed opportunities, wasted time and efforts, research methodology, ... so that they can sell more often at full price, avoid regrets in the end, open new markets focusing on real solutions, cut useless costs and research, stop wasting time on useless products that will yield nothing, avoid spending resources on unprofitable projects but on profitable ones; take their organization to a higher level, open new groundbreaking doors, boost their margins of cash and spend it on more valuable ...profits, beat their competitors; and make big profits, conserving more.

- 11. <u>**SCIENCE180 ACADEMY FOR GOVERNMENTAL AGENCIES**</u> (Do you want to know how and why most nations and governments are wasting millions of dollars on universe-origin and life-origin research they don't need … and how to avoid it? Indeed, for most developed nations, and even for some underdeveloped countries, universe-origin projects can cost billions of US dollars and other expensive things that cannot be afforded without sacrificing crucial priorities. Even in developed countries, the impact and the return on investment of the space research are subjects of intense political and economic debates. What if your nation or institution can reduce wasteful spending on universe-origin research and life-origin research, as well as your dependency on wrong theories on the origin of the universe and life? "Science180 Academy for governmental agencies" will show you how to use the latest scientific breakthrough to better understand the origin of the universe without wasting money on what is already known or what we think we don't know, but that most scientists ignore. Having spent years accurately decoding the origin of the universe, of life, and of chemicals, Dr. Nathanael-Israel Israel delivers science-backed insight to properly understand all the processes connected to the universe formation—so you don't waste more money and time on trying to research the beginning of the cosmos, but to focus on reducing the budget of spatial agencies and focus on real science, cutting-edge research, and things that inevitably lead to discovery and innovation).

- 12. **OTHER SCIENCE180 ACADEMY:** If you did not relate with any of the Science180 Academies mentioned above, but you are still interested in learning something specific about the origin of the universe, life, and chemicals that better fits your needs, please visit Science180Academy.com to contact us so we can discuss that with you.

'Science180 Academy' Success Strategy:
SCIENCE180 SERVICES AND PRODUCTS YOU OR YOUR PARENTS WILL LOVE

Because you are reading this book, you are probably very interested in answering your questions about the origin of the universe, of life, and of chemicals. Imagine you want to be trained by Dr. Nathanael-Israel Israel and his team so you can benefit from their outstanding expertise to empower yourself or your team. Or you want him to give a keynote speech, a seminar, or any other kind of talk or conference at your organization. Or you want him to mentor you or some people or teams at your organization. Maybe you have critical origin-related questions that you need his help to accurately answer. You want a true expert to talk with you about the customized program or game plan that fits your needs. You want him to tailor his advice, expert feedback, and proven shortcuts to the stage of life you are in and help you get to where you want to be in your desire to properly understand the origin of the universe, life, and chemicals and harness the benefits that come with it. Perhaps you don't know how to properly get any of these important tasks done according to your specific needs or the needs and demands of your organization. That is what Science180 Academy is all about. Visit Science180.com/services for more details about how to benefit from the services that Science180 provides.

Maybe you are a leader that wants to hire Dr. Nathanael-Israel Israel and his team to train some departments at your organization. Or you want to refer them to other companies like a good dish passed around the dinner table, and you want to explore how Nathanael-Israel Israel can pay you something for that referral. Maybe you attended Nathanael-Israel Israel's speaking program, for which, without going into details, he accurately raised your awareness about how the universe, life, and chemicals were formed.

Or maybe you attended his training, in which he detailed and showed you how he decoded the scientific data using various tools and certain thinking strategies that helped him and which transferred some skills to you; and now, you are interested in a long term one-on-one consulting, or mentoring program with him, so that, he delves into more details about how to use proven techniques to decode the universe (strategies for data collection, data analysis, data presentation, and even tips for future research) and change your behavior on a long term basis. If you relate to any of the points mentioned above, Science180 Academy is the right fit for you!

Other customizable services that Science180 provides include:

- Books and other products (e.g. booklets, online courses, posters, how-to-guides, study guides, and field guides)
- Book publishing (Yes! Science180 can publish your books!)
- Consulting
- Executive mastermind groups
- Face-to-face visits
- Podcasting
- Retreats
- Seminars
- Speaking engagements (offline and onsite—e.g., seminars, keynotes, and workshops)
- Survey and research tools
- Training
- Video programs
- Virtual presentations

Science180 is the only company that has scientifically, completely cut the rational legs upon which all God deniers, all modern freethinkers, evolutionists, and Big Bang proponents had wished to stand to continue rejecting God. Science180 is the only company that left all wrong creationist proponents, evolutionists, Big Bang advocates, and all other anti-creationists that do not literally believe the Biblical creation in an echoed silence, head-scratching and asking: "Who took our secular and religious spotlight?". To fulfill its mission, Science180 provides unconventional and holistic expertise; authoritative advice; influence; and breakthroughs on major issues concerning science and creationism through research, publication, training, education, promotion of excellent dialogue between science and faith, facilitation of the public's understanding of science, public engagement, and the dissemination of top secrets of the origin of the universe, life, and chemicals for the benefit of humanity perpetually.

Here are other reasons why you should choose to work with or hire Nathanael-Israel Israel and the team at Science180:

- A simple universe-origin and life-origin theory that made no assumption
- Accurately understand universe-origin and life-origin. Be happy forever!
- Biblical Genesis inerrancy guaranteed

- Bringing the Judeo-Christian believers together through the power of the accurate decoding and understanding of the Biblical account of creation
- Customizable universe-origin and life-origin trainings with unique materials
- Discover the key variables needed to decode the universe-origin and life-origin
- Easy-to-understand universe-origin and life-origin theory
- Enjoy scientifically verifiable, biblically based universe-origin, life-origin, and chemicals-origin models
- First stop for universe-origin and life-origin needs
- Irrefutable scientific demonstration of creation
- Nonconformist, rule-breaker, and accurate demonstrator of the universe's origin and life-origin
- Personalized universe-origin and life-origin decoding package
- Receive an exceptional universe-origin and life-origin decoding perspective
- Reuniting science and the Biblical Account of Creation
- Science and Bible reconciliation made possible
- The formula at the intersection of science and the Bible
- The go-to source for valuable universe-origin and life-origin information
- The most accurate, reliable, safest, best explanation of the universe's origin and life-origin ever
- The new physics and life-origin science that will revolutionize science forever
- The place where the universe-origin and life-origin get decoded accurately
- The science that reunites your mind and faith
- The undeniable scientific challenge to all metaphorical, figurative, loose, liberal, or vague explanations of the Biblical Creation
- The unquestionable scientific challenge to Big Bang & Evolutionism
- Trailblazer of the reconciliation between science and the Biblical account of creation
- Undeniable reconciliation of science and the Biblical account of creation

'Science180 Academy' Success Strategy
SCIENCE180 SEMINARS

People whose awareness is raised by Science180 usually ask me to go deeper or they wonder "what's else?". That is one of the reasons Science180 trains them through strategic work sessions (during seminars or training sessions) that transfer customizable skills and solutions to them. Science180 Seminars are client-centered and tailored to strongly engage the clients so they maximize the discovery of and the tapping into new opportunities, and exponentially outperform their expectations. Science180 offers customizable seminars that can be labeled as a colloquy, conference, consultation, discussion, forum, keynote speech, lecture, lesson, meeting, symposium, summit, study group, tutorial, workshop or working section accordingly on any topic related to:

- Universe-origin for scientists and mathematicians, philosophers, laypeople, and the general public
- Universe-origin or universe creation for believers
- Life-origin for life scientists, for all other scientists, and for believers
- Chemical-origin for scientists
- Universe-origin seminars for children
- Universe and life-origin for pseudepigraphic believers

As you contact us with your needs, we can customize your program accordingly. Learn more at Science180Seminars.com.

'Science180 Academy' Success Strategy
SCIENCE180 CONSULTING

Because Science180's trainings, seminars, or strategic work sessions (through which it transfers skills and training solutions) are great, some customers want to go even deeper on a long-term, sustainable basis. That is where Science180 Consulting, one-on-one consulting, and mentoring (that some people may prefer calling coaching programs) come in. That is where Science180 can truly change people's behavior on a long-term basis according to their specific needs. With Science180 Consulting, you will discover and understand the deep secrets of the formation of the universe, life, and chemicals around you. Hear Dr. Nathanael-Israel Israel's personal selection and teaching on key topics that will help you break the code of the universe's formation and functioning. All strategically designed to enlighten you, guide you to navigate and filter the massive data collected on the universe and its content so you know how to answer the world's most challenging origin questions, remove any scientific and philosophical cataracts that may be blocking you, and help bring you many steps closer to your best life today and forever. Science180 Consulting will train you, transfer unconventional skills to you, and change your behavior so you go deeper. To get started today or to learn more, go to Science180Consulting.com.

Science180: The Place Where Science Accurately Meets Biblical Creation

SECTION 14: REFERENCES AND INDEX

83. References

NASA (2018). Planetary fact sheets. Fact sheets of the Sun, planets, satellites, rings and selected asteroids in the Solar System. Author/Curator: Dr. David R. Williams, NASA Goddard Space Flight Center, Greenbelt, MD, USA. http://nssdc.gsfc.nasa.gov/planetary/factsheet/. Visited on November 19, 2018.

Israel Nathanael-Israel (2025a). Turbulent Origin of the Universe. Science180, Augusta, USA 683 pages.

Israel Nathanael-Israel (2025b). From Science to Bible's Conclusions. Science180, Augusta, USA 170 pages.

Israel Nathanael-Israel (2025c). Reconciling Science and Creation Accurately. Science180, Augusta, USA 299 pages.

Israel Nathanael-Israel (2025d). Turbulent Origin of Chemical Particles. Science180, Augusta, USA 397 pages.

Israel Nathanael-Israel (2025e). Turbulent Origin of Life. Science180, Augusta, USA 370 pages.

Israel Nathanael-Israel (2025f). Origin of the Spiritual World. Science180, Augusta, USA 151 pages.

Israel Nathanael-Israel (2025g). How Baby Universe Was Born. Science180, Augusta, USA 130 pages.

Israel Nathanael-Israel (2025h). How God Created Baby Universe. Science180, Augusta, USA 224 pages.

Israel Nathanael-Israel (2025i). Science180 Accurate Scientific Proof of God. Science180, Augusta, USA 214 pages.

84. Index

Nathanael-Israel Israel: Historic Discoverer of the Formula to Accurately Decode the Origin of the Universe, of Life, and of Chemicals in a Few Days

Nathanael-Israel Israel: Historic Discoverer of the Formula to Accurately Decode the Origin of the Universe, of Life, and of Chemicals in a Few Days

ABOUT THE AUTHOR

Dr. Nathanael-Israel Israel is the founder of Science180, the American company whose mission is to improve the current and future state of human beings by accurately decoding and teaching them the real origin and formation of the universe, of life, and of chemicals, and meaningfully engaging business, nonprofit, political, academic, civil society leaders and followers to properly shape local and global agendas that authentically value the truth. As the creator of the Universe Turbulent Origin Formula™. Dr. Nathanael-Israel Israel has revolutionized the way billions of people around the world think about the origin of the universe, of life, and of chemicals. Nobody understands and teaches the formation of everything in the universe (e.g. the Milky Way Galaxy, the Sun, the Earth, the Moon, and all other galaxies, stars, planets, satellites, and asteroids) better than Nathanael-Israel Israel. Individuals and organizations across the globe have been calling him so he helps them scientifically unlock the code of the universe's formation, -formation, helping veterans and rookies to have the real keys to decrypt the universe and turbulence (one of the top biggest unsolved mysteries in science) from the historic, unique, accurate, simple, easy-to-understand, nonconformist, trailblazing perspective that anybody can quickly learn at Science180 Academy (Science180Academy.com).

Science180 Academy delivers outstanding value, insight, and lessons to assist people to accurately understand the true origin of the universe, chemicals, and life, so they can tap into that knowledge to improve lives perpetually. Nathanael-Israel's goal is to give you practicable and undeniable proofs of the formation of the universe so you can be fired up to become the best version of you, and to cause positive changes to your initiatives that will profit you today and forever. For Nathanael-Israel, accurately decoding and teaching the origin of the universe and everything in it is not a job, but his life mission, and helping others to fully understand that brings him closer to his assignment. He is also a father who faced the same challenges of teaching his own children about the formation of the universe that most parents face.

Dr. Israel earned his PhD in Plant, Insect, and Microbial Sciences in the USA, where he graduated first of his class of hundreds of PhD candidates. This Beninese-American is a member of the American Chemical Society, American Association for

Science180: The Place Where Science Accurately Meets Biblical Creation

the Advancement of Science, American Society of Agricultural and Biological Engineers, American Society for Microbiology, American Society of Biochemistry and Molecular Biology, Ecological Society of America, American Society of Agronomy, Crop Science Society of America, and Soil Science Society of America.

A scientist, a mathematician, a consultant, and the owner of a news company in the USA, Dr. Israel is the author of the popular books:

- Turbulent Origin of Chemical Particles
- Turbulent Origin of Life
- From Science to Bible's Conclusions
- How Baby Universe Was Born
- How God Created Baby Universe
- Science180 Accurate Scientific Proof of God
- Turbulent Origin of the Universe
- Reconciling Science and Creation Accurately
- Origin of the Spiritual World
- Mathematical Proof of God's Existence at the Intersection of Science and Faith
- Boldest Scientific Formula of God and Creation

If you want to accurately understand the origin of anything, then be sure to get a copy of these amazing books. You cannot afford to ignore the greater, better, faster, simpler, cheaper, easier, and accurate formulas unlocked in these important books that successfully cracked the origin of the universe, of life, and of chemicals in a language that scientists, laypeople, adults, children, believers, skeptics, and anybody else can properly understand and enjoy.

Visit Israel120.com today to connect with this historic discoverer of the all-in-one, proven, and uncomplicated formula that accurately decoded the origin of the universe, of life, and of chemicals.

For any suggestions or questions, please visit Science180.com/contact and Nathanael-Israel Israel's personal website: Israel120.com. Feel free to ask any questions you have about the universe formation, life formation, and chemical formation.

Nathanael-Israel Israel: Known as the #1 International Authority that Truly Unlocked the Secrets of the Turbulence that Shaped the Universe

www.ingramcontent.com/pod-product-compliance
Lightning Source LLC
Chambersburg PA
CBHW070912130626
46555CB00001B/105